Lecture Notes in Computer Science

Lecture Notes in Computer Science

Edited by G. Goos and J. Hartmanis

103

Henry Ledgard
Andrew Singer
John Whiteside

Directions in Human Factors
for Interactive Systems

Springer-Verlag
Berlin Heidelberg New York 1981

Authors

Henry Ledgard
Dept. of Computer and Information Science
University of Massachusetts
Amherst, USA

Andrew Singer
E and L Instruments Corporation
Derby, Connecticut, 06418 USA

John Whiteside
Digital Equipment Corporation
Maynard, Massachusetts, USA

AMS Subject Classifications (1979): –
CR Subject Classifications (1979):   2.1, 3.8, 2.4

ISBN 3-540-10574-3 Springer-Verlag Berlin Heidelberg New York
ISBN 0-387-10574-3 Springer-Verlag New York Heidelberg Berlin

Preface

This monograph contains a series of articles on a common theme, human factors for interactive systems. There is no question that this area, somewhat neglected in the past, is emerging as a vital need in the development of computer technology. We are committed to the belief that there are giant strides to be made in tailoring software to the human user.

This monograph is organized in two major parts. The first part, Chapters 1 through 4, discusses issues in the design of interactive systems. By "interactive" we mean any system where the user and a computer engage in a dialogue. The second part, Chapter 5 through 8, discusses the design of experiments. Ultimately, validation of any design principle requires that it be tested, and experimentation is beginning to play an important role in computer science.

Knowledge of human factors for computer systems is clearly in its infancy. As such, the work discussed here presents some first steps.

Much of this work mentions the use of text editors. This particular application is incidental to our intent. We believe that with a few exceptions, many of the ideas presented here generalize to the design of any interactive system. There has been a tendency in the past to view results from a particular application, text editing for example, as being relevant only to that area. For this work we can only say that text editing is simply one application of the principles we discuss.

Four references are particularly germane to this work. Ramsey and Atwood [1979] present a comprehensive annotated bibliography of computer science work related to human factors in software. Schneiderman [1980] provides a text in the area of software psychology. Gilb and Weinberg [1977] present a model human factors guide for the design of keyed data input systems. Andrew Singer's thesis [1979] forms the foundation of much that is written here.

For acknowledgments, we are especially grateful to the National Science Foundation, who funded this work. William Seymour conducted the earlier phases of the experiment mentioned in Chapter 5 and was mainly responsible for the development of its diary in Chapter 6. Jon Hueras actively participated in the design of the Pascal Assistant and encouraged our thinking in human factors. Michael Marcotty gave thoughtful advice during all phases of this work. Lance Miller and Rudy Ramsey provided thoughtful criticism. Rich Scire did the special programming for the experiment discussed in Chapter 5. Conrad Wogrin and the University of Massachusetts Computing Center provided support for this research.

Henry Ledgard
Andrew Singer
John Whiteside

Contents

Experiments

This work was supported by the National Science Foundation

Chapter 1

The Case for Human Engineering

In the development of any technology there is always a tendency to lose sight of the basic problems that stimulated its introduction. After the first flush of success, interest naturally tends to focus on the technology itself and the problems it presents. We often forget that the original objective of computer technology is not just to develop more powerful systems but to *increase the overall effectiveness of a human problem solver.*

The literature indicates that we have been preoccupied with the technology rather than the users. Works on the design of programs, machines, languages, and algorithms abound. By contrast, works that address the human factors of computing are rare, although thankfully beginning to emerge.

In a similar vein, the recent spate of research in software quality has concentrated on programming techniques, validation, management of large systems, and reliability. All these are aimed at producing better quality systems; yet none of them *directly* addresses the problem of producing systems that are easier to use. Surely no one would argue that ease of use is not a factor in the "quality" of software.

The work described here has proceeded from the general assumption that the study of human-computer interaction can make a significant contribution to the design of interactive systems. Interacting with a computer can be a complex and demanding intellectual activity. Some of the complexity is inherent in the nature of computing, but much results from the lack of design principles that are informed by knowledge of human capabilities, limitations, and preferences.

We consider here the design of interactive systems, that is, any system where a user and a computer engage in a dialogue. Designing such a system involves many decisions about which capabilities to include, what sequences of operations to allow, and so on. Our concern is that designers have available to them deep-rooted design principles motivated by concern for the convenience, efficiency, and comfort of the eventual user.

Although meager, there has been some work directed at better human engineering of computer systems. This research has generally fallen into three categories: applications to specific designs, experiments on specific issues, and artificial intelligence.

In the first category, there have been several attempts to produce well human engineered systems. A good example is the work of Wilcox et al. [1976]. The authors developed an on-line system that aids a user in finding errors in programs. The system allows a user to scan erroneous statements and obtain suggestions on possible errors. Furthermore, the authors make effective use of the PLATO terminal to give a user graphically annotated copies of program fragments. This kind of concern is much in the spirit of the ideas discussed here.

In the second category, there are a growing number of experiments designed to test certain features of computer systems. An example is a very early experiment reported in [Sackman 1970]. This work describes an unusual experiment in which one subject, Sackman himself, used a self-tutoring manual for the TINT interpretive language. He had never used the system before and followed the self-tutoring manual completely for each lesson. During the experiment, he recorded his errors and documented his attitude toward the method. He observed that typing errors appeared at a constant rate, despite his knowledge of the system. He also noted the tendency toward fatigue and boredom with the self-tutoring method and suggested that complete reliance on self-tutoring is too extreme a method to use.

In the third category, there is work in artificial intelligence. Research in artificial intelligence is often directed at providing a very high level interface to the user. Typical topics include the development of adaptive systems and the use of natural languages. While these issues certainly can have a great impact on the kind of human interface that computer systems can provide, not enough thought has been given to the constraints imposed by human limitations. What if, as a paper by Thomas and Gould [1975] seems to suggest, natural language is not the best interface? How rapidly should systems adapt? When do the capabilities that a system provides exceed a person's ability to manage them? The answers to these questions depend intrinsically on human, not machine, capabilities.

1.1 The User's Dilemma

Consider the following innocuous looking command:

REN[UM] [starting-number / *10*]   [increment / *starting-number*]

taken from a typical system allowing line-numbered files. Brackets delimit optional items. REN is an allowed abbreviation for RENUM, which is itself an abbreviation for the English word "renumber." In the first field, 10 is the default starting line number. In the second field, the starting line number is the default increment between line numbers.

Let us begin by examining the abbreviation. In using an on-line system with a typewriter keyboard, abbreviations are critical to the rapid input of correct commands. On many systems there is no uniform abbreviation rule. Some keywords can be abbreviated by their first letter, others by two letters, still others by three, and some not at all. The user is thus forced to remember a detailed set of individual abbreviations. Our experience indicates that users respond to this situation in a variety of ways. Some make the effort to remember each abbreviation. Others just type commands out in full. Some try guessing at a general rule. Many bring their manuals to the terminal. None escape without paying in some way for the awkward abbreviation scheme.

Next consider the syntax of the command. Typically, command formats force the user to remember subtly different, order-dependent fields. Such forms are error prone and distracting.

A large number of psycholinguistic experiments suggest that all aspects of human information processing are highly trained by natural language experience. We believe that interactive languages should be closely modeled after familiar phrase structures to take advantage of such training. A syntax like

RENUMBER [FROM *starting-number*]   [INCREMENTING BY *number*]

(where the individual phrases may appear in any order) or an entirely different approach like

START WITH *number*
INCREMENT BY *number*
RENUMBER

(where assumptions like START and INCREMENT are remembered by the system) takes advantage of established language habits. An appropriate

Table 1.1 Some Common Complaints

1. *The language or system is too large.* In an attempt to provide all things to all users, the language or system becomes so large that its complexity acts as a barrier to the user.

2. *The documentation or terminology is incomprehensible.* Most users of computer systems are not computer scientists by training, yet the documentation or terminology they must use is written in the vocabulary of the computer expert.

3. *The system provides no warning of a potentially dangerous action.* It is often possible to destroy hours of valuable work through a single erroneous operation.

4. *Language forms are difficult to remember.* The syntax of each form has been individually designed to optimize some local goal, often minimal keystrokes. As a result, the system's language is unsystematic and thus difficult to learn and remember.

5. *Abbreviation rules are not uniform.* In an attempt to improve the ease of use, abbreviations are permitted. However, without a consistent rule, the saving in keystrokes is lost to the effort of remembering the right one.

6. *Messages are often cryptic.* Like the documentation, the system messages use the vocabulary of the computer expert and are often terse to the point of obscurity. While a short message may save printing time and be sufficient for the expert user, it offers the typical user little assistance.

7. *Users are unable to communicate their difficulties to the designers.* Many expert system designers soon forget their early experiences and frustrations. The systems they design show this, and without the feedback from typical users, there can be little hope for improvement.

8. *Error creation is easy.* Languages are designed with little consideration for the weaknesses of human information processing. For example, in some systems, users must be able to count commas visually, a task that few can perform reliably.

9. *Error correction is difficult.* Users, especially novices, inevitably make mistakes. The system often does little to help the user understand an error or to assist in its correction.

Table 1.1 (continued)

---

10. *The system provides redundant forms of the same operation.* Several methods of achieving the same result are often provided. The user is thus confused by subtle or nonexistent differences between methods.

11. *The system requires that users learn much irrelevant information.* In the attempt to do everything for all users, most users must learn about features that are of little relevance.

12. *Assistance features are not an integral part of the system.* While the need for user assistance has often been recognized, few truly usable automatic mechanisms have been developed.

13. *Many useful tasks are not automated.* Most systems provide elaborate facilities for file conversion, compilation, data base management, as well as libraries for sophisticated tasks. Yet common tasks like file preservation or the undoing of an erroneous action are seldom automated.

---

abbreviation rule for either of these approaches might be to abbreviate any word by its first letter.

Finally, there are a number of general issues that need to be resolved. Should a renumbering command be fully automatic and not require user-specified options? Should files be based on line numbers at all? If so, what should the defaults be? Should the line numbers be considered part of the file during compilation?

These are all difficult problems. Yet in every system there are a myriad of such minor "details." From the user's point of view, these details are often the most frequently encountered consequences of the design. For example, the prompting signals given the user by a system are encountered in every interaction, while a highly specialized command may only be used once in a session, or perhaps not at all. It's the little things in life that count because we experience them again and again. Clearly many of these apparently insignificant details are critical design issues and may have far greater impact on users than some of the "large" design decisions.

Table 1.1 summarizes some typical problems with almost every system that we have encountered. Solving these problems is far from easy, but they are as pervasive as computer technology itself.

1.2 Complexity Due to Scale

Every item in Table 1.1 deserves extensive discussion. We touch here on one item we believe to be the most critical symptom of poor human engineering: complexity due to scale. We enumerate below some consequences that result when a system is overly large and complex.

The effort to promote the system is resisted. The success of any effort depends upon its perception by its users. When a system is perceived to be large and thus threatening, there is a clear tendency to avoid it. While it may be argued that there is resistance to any new technology, an effort to promote a system that is perceived to be complex can only result in a strong undercurrent of reluctance to adopt or try it. It is rare to find any potential user without reservations about the scale and complexity of a system.

Tutorial documents can readily become incomprehensible. The successful teaching of a new system to potential users is vital to its acceptance. When a system becomes large, the development of good tutorials becomes increasingly difficult. If the entire system is to be covered, the tutorial can become so long that even its physical length is a deterrent to the user. If only a portion of the system is covered, there then comes the question of which features to exclude. If features are excluded, the student may be left wondering if, in fact, there isn't something else that must be learned and that might be vital to a problem.

If we further accept the idea that writing of tutorials is an imperfectly developed art, then complexity and scale can only make the likelihood of a poorly written document higher. Furthermore, the introduction of any new system inevitably requires the introduction of more terminology. When the number of new ideas introduced is great, the student can become readily overwhelmed.

Implementation becomes increasingly difficult. There is no question that the larger the system the more difficult the implementation. A system that is simple to implement often carries its own grassroots support. Consider the success of Basic, a language supported by a small interactive environment. This language has thrived despite any significant commercial or federal support. Subsets of the underlying system are rare, and new implementations keep sprouting up.

Implementations become prone to error. It would be nice to imagine a perfect world in which every implementation mirrored the product exactly. Such is far from the case. As a system becomes larger and larger, the potential for errors in the implementation grows, with newly issued versions that supposedly correct the errors. Claims to a complete implementation become virtually impossible. There is no question that almost every commercial system has been plagued by the problem of errors. Even in relatively small word-processing systems, this is the case as well.

Diagnostic messages can easily become misleading. There is no question that the larger the system, the larger the number and variety of diagnostic messages. An implementation can never know the scope of the user's knowledge. Furthermore, the implementation, made with full knowledge of the entire system, can only give diagnostic advice in the larger terms of the system as a whole. Such messages may often be cryptic to the user who does not share this full knowledge.

Standardization efforts become virtually impossible. The development of tight legal standards is important to the success of any effort. Such efforts are never easy. The need for rigorous terminology, the phrasing of sentences, and the need to cover absolutely every possible system construct make any effort, even for small systems, a tedious undertaking.

We have all seen the difficulties in attempting to standardize any interactive system, even that supported by a single vendor. On this front, there is absolutely no question that the smaller the system the more likely the success of promoting a standard version.

Side by side with standardization efforts stand the efforts to validate any proposed implementation. The same arguments for standardization apply to validation. Here, however, the problem is compounded by the need to provide mechanical ways of ensuring that the language conforms to a given specification. Validation efforts can be very expensive, and the larger the system the more expensive the validation.

The tendency towards subsetting becomes almost irresistible. At a certain point, systems become sufficiently complex that user groups tend to develop their own subsets. As a result, different subsets are promoted by different groups, and some of these subsets even evolve into their own nonstandard dialects. Such efforts can only hamper communication between users and the portability of their work.

Language forms become overloaded. With the development of any large system, there is a strong tendency during design to "combine" features. In CMS [IBM, 1976], for example, various file types, file modes, as well as line-numbered files are handled with common commands. While at first this appears to be a simplification, the commands become overloaded with different meanings in different contexts. Such a tendency promotes subtle and often treacherous distinctions that must be made by the user.

Language forms become difficult to remember. As a system becomes larger and larger, the choice of forms that a user must draw from to solve a problem becomes greater and greater. Remembering all of these forms becomes increasingly difficult. Often the user is left with no choice but to head for the manual.

Error creation becomes easier. A human's information processing capabilities are limited. Only so much information can be absorbed and used effectively. When information is incomplete, as is likely to be the case in using a large system, the creation of errors becomes all too easy.

We are not talking here only of diagnosed punctuation or spelling errors, but also of that larger and much more subtle source of errors that have traditionally plagued users: commands that do not perform as expected. The larger the system the more difficult it is to make a given construct correct and to comprehend it well even when it finally is correct.

The development of automated tools becomes complex and expensive. Most systems are supported with elaborate facilities for file conversion, program libraries, verification aids, and what have you. Every designer of every such tool must face the consequences of the entire system in providing such tools. With a large system, such efforts can often become extremely time consuming and expensive.

The development of a conceptual model for using the system becomes virtually impossible. There is no question that users perform best when they have a clear model of the entire system that they are using. This model provides a guide for selecting constructs and using them judiciously.

As a system becomes larger and larger, the development of such a model becomes increasingly difficult. More features must be integrated into the model, areas in the language may not be understood, and many aspects of the language may not be fully understood. Such problems interfere with the user's almost subconscious search for something simple to go by. When a simple model is not developed, correct usage becomes chancy, and clear instructions become increasingly more difficult to devise.

And what is the cumulative effect of all of these problems?

Complexity of scale is a burden to everyone.

The entire effort is slowed, acceptance by the user community is undermined, and the costs become greater and greater.

1.3 The Costs of Poor Human Engineering

The costs that result from a poorly human engineered system are more difficult to assess than the cost of the system itself. It is easy to measure central processor time, disk space, and input-output capacity. Nevertheless, while human costs are less obvious, they may be staggering. Moreover, while hardware costs have seen drastic reductions, the cost of human time has continued to escalate.

We see four areas where the costs of poor human engineering are evident: direct costs, indirect costs, human suffering, and limited use. We believe that the last is by far the most expensive.

Direct costs

Direct costs are easy to point out. Poor designs often lead to wasted human time at a terminal, as well as wasted computer time. How often have we seen a user receive an unusual but cryptic message, and try over and over again to repeat a sequence of commands in an attempt to skirt the message? The simple omission to save a file may cost hours. And what of the excessive file duplication to which users resort to prevent such inadvertent losses?

We have all paid our share of direct costs. How many remember an aborted program run, searching through core dumps (the nadir of human engineering), retrials, rethinking, searching for system bugs, and more trials, just because of a simple mistake? How nice it would have been to be warned of the possibility of error in the first place.

Indirect costs

In this area, we lump a large number of indirect costs. By "indirect" we mean not associated with direct machine use, but rather with the day-to-day problems on the periphery of man-machine encounters.

There are perhaps hundreds of indirect, cost-related issues. We list but a few:

- the time spent in understanding the vocabulary of a system,

- the cost of printing excessive documentation,

- the time spent in understanding manuals,

- the time spent in learning abbreviations,

- the time spent in mastering system formats,

- the lateness of projects caused by having to deal with a difficult system,

- the lack in communication of ideas among users,

- the time spent in understanding errors,

- the mental overhead in remembering duplicate forms,

- the manual costs of features that should have been automated.

These costs apply to any interactive system, no matter what the application. Unfortunately, most users and most designers of most systems take for granted that *their* system is an *exception*. This is seldom the case.

Human Suffering

The third area, which we call human suffering, is more subtle. By this we mean the class of negative psychological effects associated with the use of a system. The frustration that results from repeated mistakes due to some error prone feature of a system is one example. Another is the anxiety that results when a system appears to behave erratically. Yet another is the pressure and fatigue caused by frequent difficulties in understanding system responses, dealing with irregular behavior, and keeping track of mentally difficult exercises that systems demand.

Of course there is no reasonable way one can put any cost estimates on these kinds of problems. Nonetheless, they are some of the worst consequences of our profession, and we pay for them. In some instances, these costs may be so great that no individual can really evaluate them.

Limited Use

In the last area, we come to what we believe is *the* major cost of poor human engineering. Indeed, all the foregoing problems can only force us to conclude that:

There are many people who should, but do not, use computers.

Chapter 2

General Design Issues

In this chapter we discuss a number of broad design considerations for interactive languages. It is important to bear in mind that our knowledge of what constitutes a "good" decision from a human factors point of view is rather primitive. Often our only guide is intuition based on experience. Ultimately, results of experimental investigations in psychology and human engineering experiments in computing will provide a solid basis for designs. This issue will be discussed later in the text.

As an example of an interactive system, we shall consider some of the editing commands associated with the CMS editor [IBM 1976]. These commands are summarized in Table 2.1. This system is often perceived as easy to use, and represents one of the better commercially available designs.

2.1 Dealing with Complexity

The complexity and scale of a system depends markedly on the intended application. When the scale is too small, the system primitives become so overloaded that the user is constantly searching for cryptic combinations to solve a given problem. When the size is too large, all the problems mentioned earlier arise. There are few interactive systems that do not, in fact, suffer from undue size and attendant complexity. Even with the popularity of word processors, supposedly designed for the layperson, complexity of scale is rampant.

Table 2.1 Partial Summary of CMS Editing Subcommands

Italics specify default parameters. Square brackets enclose optional items. Vertical bars separate alternative choices. Uppercase letters denote keywords. Lowercase letters denote user-supplied variables.

Format	*Function*
AL[TER] char1 char2 [*1*	n	* [G	*]]	Scan the next n records of the file, altering the specified character, either once in each line or for all occurrences in the line.
AUTO[SAVE] [n	*OFF*]	Automatically save the current file every n changes or additions.
BA[CKWARD] [*1*	n]	Move the current line pointer n lines backward.
B[OTTOM]	Make the last line of the file the current line.
C[HANGE] [/str1 [/str2 [/*1*	n [G	*]]]	Change string-1 to string-2 for n records or to the EOF, either for the first occurrence in each line or for all occurrences.
CMS	Return to CMS subset command mode.
DEL[ETE] [*1*	n	*]	Delete n lines or to the end of the file (*).
DO[WN] [*1*	n]	Move the current line pointer n lines ahead.
DS[TRING] /[string [/]]	Delete all lines from the current line down to the line containing the indicated string.
FILE [fn]	Save the file being edited on disk or change its identifiers. Return to CMS.
F[IND] [line]	Search the file for the given line.
FN[AME] [fn]	Reset or display the filename.
FO[RWARD] [*1*	n]	Point to the n-th line after the current line.
G[ETFILE] fn [*1*	m [*	n]]	Insert a portion or all of the specified file after the current line.
I[NPUT] [line]	Insert a line in the file or enter input mode.
LINE[MODE] [LEFT	RIGHT	OFF]	Line numbers are inserted on the left or right, or are not used. With no argument, display line mode setting.
[L[OCATE]] /[string[/]]	Scan file from next line for first occurrence of the string.
LONG	Enter long error message mode.
N[EXT] [*1*	n]	Point to the n-th line down from the current line.

O[VERLAY] [line]	Replace all or part of the current line.
PROMPT [*10* | n]	Set or display line number increment; initial setting is 10.
QUIT	Terminate edit session with no updates incorporated since last save request.
REN[UM] [*10* | m [m | n]]	Recompute line numbers for VSBASIC and FREEFORT source files, beginning with m and incrementing by n.
REPEAT [*1* | n | *]	Execute the following OVERLAY subcommand n times.
R[EPLACE] [line]	Replace the current line or delete the current line and enter input mode.
RES[TORE]	Restore Editor settings to values last preserved.
RETURN	Return to edit environment from CMS subset.
SAVE [fn]	Save the file on disk and stay in edit environment.
[REUSE | =]	Stack the last issued subcommand for subsequent reuse.
SHORT	Enter short error message mode.
TABS[ET] n1 [n2 ... nn]	Set logical tab stops.
TOP	Move the current line pointer to the null line at the top of the file.
TRUNC [n | *]	Set or display the column of truncation. A * indicates the logical record length.
T[YPE] [*1* | m | * [n | *]]	Display m lines beginning with the current line. Each line may be truncated to n characters.
U[P] [*1* | n]	Move the current line pointer toward the top of the file.
V[ERIFY] [*ON* | OFF] [[*1* | startcol] * | endcol]	Set, display, or reset verification. A * indicates the logical record length.
Z[ONE] [*1* | m | * [n | *]]	Set or display the columns m through n between which editing is to take place.
?	Display the last EDIT subcommand, except for a ? subcommand.
nnnnn [text]	Locate the line specified by the given line number and insert text, if given.
$DUP [*1* | n]	Duplicate the current line n times. $DUP is an edit macro.

Dealing with complexity is much more difficult than talking about its consequences. The ultimate solution is to produce *better designs*, and this is the general topic of this work. However, we shall first make a number of points dealing only with scaling down an existing design.

Perhaps the first line of attack is simply living without certain features. Any serious attempt to live without a given feature is bound to give rise to criticism. It is much easier to add than to remove a feature from a design. Someone will inevitably have a vested interest in the feature being deleted, and this voice will often give rise to criticism.

One candidate for deletion to the CMS editor would be the option for line numbered editing. A fundamental issue in text editing is the basic unit of information around which editing is oriented. CMS allows two completely different orientations: line numbers, and text. It is generally accepted that a text orientation provides a much more powerful and useful means of editing text. Searching for a given string, replacement of text fragments, and the concept of a "current line" are commonplace with this approach.

With the line numbered approach, the lines of a file are associated with line numbers. Thus it is possible to search for a line with a given line number or to renumber the lines. This is a clear case of duplicate methods for achieving the same result. Admittedly, languages like Basic, where line numbers are intrinsic to the text, pose a special case. But in the main, line-numbered editing is not particularly satisfying. The line numbers have very little to do with the content of the text, and pose an additional mental burden on the user. We thus suggest that deleting this feature would be a valuable contribution to simplicity.

Next consider the ALTER request. This request allows changes to be made to a single character. While not illustrated in the table, the ALTER command also allows characters to be specified by their hexadecimal values. This feature is obviously analogous to the CHANGE request. Its inclusion in the editor is dubious. Presumably, the additional facility to enter hexadecimal values could be incorporated into the CHANGE command if needed.

Next, notice that the DOWN, FORWARD, and NEXT commands, each move the line pointer ahead, and both the CMS and FILE commands cause exit from the editor.

Consider also the OVERLAY request. This command allows the replacement of characters in a line by spacing the terminal's typing element to a particular character position and then making character by character replacements. This request is obviously a duplicate feature, functionally similar to the CHANGE request. On screen-oriented editors, an overlay-like feature can indeed be both powerful and useful. However, within the context of typewriter based terminals that CMS was designed to support, the OVERLAY request is not especially useful. Character deletions usually associated with replacements are cumbersome. Unless such a feature is accompanied by other features often found in word processing systems, the overlay feature poses yet another candidate for possible deletion.

The overlay feature brings up a serious point about compressing the concepts for typewriter-based editors with screen-oriented editors. It may well be argued that these two devices are intrinsically so different that they warrant entirely different design strategies.

There are other possibilities for cuts to the CMS editor. Of course, when the chips are down, making the actual deletions is a hard decision. Nevertheless, for good human engineering we must be able to do more with fewer features.

As mentioned above, the most critical technique for keeping the scale of the system to a minimum is the development of a comprehensive design approach in the first place. Simple design ideas are at the heart of any attempt to keep the scale to a minimum. In Chapter 3, we present a system somewhat similar in its purpose to the CMS editor. We shall see in this example a number of different ideas for expressing similar interactive capabilities.

2.2 Abbreviation Rules

In every interactive system the user must give instructions to carry out requests. The ideal, of course, would be to have special keys for each conceptual function; but the real world of ordinary terminals precludes this approach.

Consider the following CMS abbreviations:

```
C       for     CHANGE
DO      for     DOWN
TOP     for     TOP
DEL     for     DELETE
```

The strategy for abbreviation in the CMS editor is basically that of allowing the user to abbreviate any keyword by one or more initial letters, where the initial letters differentiate the abbreviated form from any other possible abbreviated forms. This is certainly a simple abbreviation approach to understand. However, underlying this strategy is the subtle assumption that the user can keep track of all initial letter sequences required for abbreviation. This is a poor assumption to make. Few users can remember all of the request names, let alone their abbreviations. Many users will be forced to remember individual abbreviations for each keyword. This kind of abbreviation thus seems far from satisfactory.

A solution to this problem is the adoption of other, more uniform, abbreviation rules. Furthermore, abbreviated forms should be able to be typed without intervening spaces. The goal is to allow abbreviated forms that are easy to formulate and fast to type. The user should be able to think in the long form, while typing an abbreviated form.

An approach to abbreviations is not a "minor" issue. One of the least thought out philosophies of almost every system we have seen is its abbreviation strategy. Abbreviations, like other so-called "details" of design, are often critical to the effective use of an interactive system.

We take the extreme position of supporting abbreviation by initial letter. From the user's point of view, the first letter abbrevation rule is very powerful, since the input of user requests can be terse and simple. From a designer's point of view, this convention can be difficult to live with, for it forces keywords to have different first letters. In the CMS case, this would call for a drastic redesign of syntax, which is called for on other grounds as well.

An argument commonly advanced against terse abbreviation rules is that designers cannot easily expand the keyword list, i.e. add new requests. In rebuttal, we would suggest that such add-ons would be best accomplished by a complete redesign if all the interlocking design aspects are to receive the consideration they deserve. Furthermore, any keywords *within* a request are free from conflict from keywords within other requests.

2.3   Correction of Errors

One of our fundamental assumptions is that a system should accommodate easy correction of errors. User errors generally fall into one of three categories:

1.   Typing errors that lead to ill-formed requests, for example, typing

    LOCAKE /NOW IS THE TIME/

where the K should be a T.

2.   Typing or judgment errors that lead to a request that cannot be fully carried out, for example, saying

    DOWN 100

where 100 should be 10 and there are not 100 lines in the edited file.

3.   Judgment errors that lead to a meaningful but unintended result, for example, saying

    CHANGE /C/B/ 100

where there are at least 100 occurrences of C in the edited file, but the C should be an A.

CMS provides no particular assistance in each of the three cases.

For the first kind of error (a diagnosed syntax error), every system allows the user to respond by entering a revised request. For lengthy requests this is a poor solution. An alternative that we strongly recommend is a facility to edit request lines just as text itself is edited. For example, suppose a user inadvertently types

```
LOCAKE /NOW IS THE TIME/
```

in order to move to the line containing "NOW IS THE TIME." A simple request correction like /K/T/ to change K to T, followed by an automatic re-issue of the corrected request, results in a considerable saving of time.

This correction feature is especially useful in editors that allow compound requests, i.e. multiple requests on a single line. Many users often avoid this feature in fear of a likely typing error that might invalidate (and thus cause retyping) a long and carefully formulated compound request. The correction feature considerably relieves this problem.

For the second case (a request that cannot be fully carried out), the solution is more difficult. Automatically performing a partially completed request may be unwise, since the user may have made an error. On the other hand, reporting a recoverable error may be just as unwise, since the partial completion of the request may be just what was originally intended.

We believe the right solution here is a confirmation or "security check," asking the user whether to go ahead or not. The problem with this solution is an implementation question, since confirming that a request cannot be completely performed requires execution of the request. A negative answer to the security check requires undoing the partially completed request. If a potential error is discovered and the security check confirms the error, the request can be secretly undone. (An Undo feature is discussed below.)

This philosophy of security checking is not novel, but is not common-place. In addition to security checks for requests that cannot be fully carried out, any attempt to overwrite files should also be checked. Thus, the user is always given a chance to think twice before going ahead. As Gilb and Weinberg [1977] point out, at times and for some users, automatic protection and forced interaction may be a nuisance. One solution to this problem is a request that allows the user to suppress security checks or at least minimize their use.

The third type of error (a meaningful but unintended request) is potentially *far* more damaging to the user. Usually, after the response from the system, the user may discover that his intent was wrong. In many systems, a user may just have to face the error. One solution to this problem is the use of an explicit undo request, i.e. one that erases the effect of one or more previous requests. Like the immediate request correction feature, it allows the user to recover easily from certain kinds of errors.

An undo feature, however, poses some especially difficult implementation problems. An undo can be effected by retaining two copies of the user's state, one of which is the version existing at some earlier time. Furthermore, before executing new requests, a copy of this state can be made to preserve the original state. Although simple, this is an "expensive" solution, requiring storage space for two versions and execution time for copying the complete state at periodic intervals.

Effective solutions to the undo problem are not easy to devise. Further, if the undo mechanism is secretly used when the user confirms an error during a security check, the frequency of undo's can be quite high. It might be acceptable to have "expensive" solutions to this problem if the price were paid only when an undo is explicitly invoked.

2.4   User Dialogue

One particularly confusing feature of CMS, as well as most interactive languages, is the notation used to enter requests. Consider the following commands

AUTOSAVE 10	— Automatically saves file every 10 changes
CHANGE /APPLE/PEAR/	— Changes "APPLE" to "PEAR"
FIND PEACH	— Searches for " PEACH" beginning a line
LOCATE /PEACH/	— Searches for next occurrence of "PEACH"
=	— Retries LOCATE request from top of file
DELETE *	— Deletes all remaining lines
$DUP 3	— Duplicates the current line 3 times
00460 PEACH	— Puts " PEACH" on line 00460

Notice that AUTOSAVE is not a verb, the CHANGE request does not make it clear that APPLE is changed to PEAR (and not the other way around), and FIND has no string delimiters. The = sign is hardly mnemonic, and the ubiquitous * is suppose to mean "all."

What is lacking here is a simple, uniform strategy for the design of requests, and we explore this issue in much greater detail in Chapter 5. We now turn to the question of system responses.

In any interactive system there are several modes for user responses; for example, modes where the user must enter a request, where a user must enter text, or where the user must confirm or deny the execution of another request. Many systems give a uniform prompting signal for these modes, for example, a "?", "/", or a space. Unfortunately, uniform prompts often leave a user guessing as to what is required.

This problem is compounded by several apparently unrelated features. For one, the system must give response messages back to the user. Further, lines of text from the user's file must often be displayed, and the printing of text lines must be used as a guide for input of new text. If the prefixes for prompting and for display of system responses are not of uniform length, alignment of new text with existing text can become confusing. Furthermore, prompting signals and message prefixes should give some indication of their role and should not normally conflict with text that the user may supply. This situation typifies the interlocking of design details and the depth to which attention must be given.

One reasonable solution to this problem is illustrated below:

Prompt Response Expected

--	Request
++	New text input
//	Security check

Prefix System Display

**	A message
bb	Text listing

where b indicates a blank. The use of two (rather than 1) prompting characters is intended to make reading the session dialogue more transparent.

We bring up this issue to illustrate a vital point. Something as apparently innocuous as prompting signals and message prefixes are an important design concern, simply because they effect *every* transaction between the system and the user.

2.5 The Help Key

If there is one feature that would be desirable in all systems, no matter how complex, it is a facility of on-line user assistance. The all too frequent user dilemma goes something like this:

The user is proceeding along with his interactive dialogue. Matters go smoothly for a while, and then some discrepancy arises. The user is not quite sure what has happened or may not be sure of what to do. The manual is of little help, for the user's predicament is highly dependent upon the kind of work actually done. Frustration and a great loss of time result.

The concept of on-line user assistance is certainly not novel. Yet most systems that have such a feature suffer from a great many defects.

Unfortunately, the issue of on-line assistance can pose some rather severe implementation problems and we make no pretext of solving these problems. Yet with all our sophisticated compilers, numeric and simulation packages, and complicated operating systems, it is unfortunate that such an important facility as on-line assistance has received but scant attention.

The failure to recognize the importance of user assistance is especially costly. Vast amounts of money have been spent on optimization of machine resources, and the cost of machines has been decreasing dramatically as well. Yet human resources, always increasing in cost, have received but small investments.

We offer here a few guidelines for the development of any viable on-line assistance facility. Our philosophy is motivated by imagining a single key on the terminal with HELP written on it. At any time in which the user is in trouble, the user may press this key and be given assistance. We now turn to some issues in designing such a HELP key.

First, and foremost the user should be able to press this key at *any* time during an interactive dialogue. This is a sweeping requirement. The user may have just finished a simple request to display lines of a text, or on the other hand, may have just received an error message that cannot be deciphered. The user may be uncertain of the status of his files, or may be inputting text to a new file and now is unsure how to terminate the input of new text. Such a far reaching range of requirements certainly pose tough implementation difficulties.

Second, the user should also be able to provide pertinent information. Often the user wishes information on some item relevant to the problem at hand. Unlike a simple menu prompting system, where keys to the new information are provided by the system, the user may have a particular item in mind that he wishes the assistance on. Obviously, user-provdied keys require some kind of dictionary facility within the on-line assistance mechanism. Yet for steering the user quickly to the resolution of a problem, the use of dictionary information is essential.

Third, the system should be able to provide prompts (or menus) to guide the user in the search for information. Menu prompting is commonplace in many interactive systems. As a general interactive strategy pervasive throughout a user dialogue, we disagree with this view. We take the view that menu prompts should only be provided when the user requests them. This can be easily incorporated into the HELP key facility. In fact, we believe that this is precisely the time when prompts are needed. When things are going smoothly, menu prompting can often be a burden. But when general assistance is sought, prompting can be invaluable.

Finally, the assistance facility should keep track of previous requests. Often a user's difficulty is related to a sequence of actions that have somehow gone astray. The on-line assistance facility should be able to inform the user of the actions that he has previously taken in order to help the user understand how to remedy the situation.

2.6 Some Special Aspects of Text Editing

One of the most fundamental issues in text editing is the basic unit of information around which editing is oriented. Some editors are oriented around the concept of a "current line," some are "character based" (that is, the user's position in the file may occur in the middle of a line), others are "page oriented" (that is, interaction is always in terms of multiple lines of text). Obviously, the kind of terminals in use and the kind of text to be edited enter into this issue. For example, CMS is basically designed around a moderate speed (10-30 cps), typewriter-based terminal. Furthermore, it was designed primarily to edit computer programs. The editing of normal prose gives rise to even greater problems.

Most editors based on the "current line" concept suffer from the drawback that the user must mentally keep track of what the current line is. This defect results from an inconsistent strategy with respect to line pointer movement. We believe that the current line should *always* be the last line seen by the user. This is the general strategy used in the CMS editor. The advantage of this strategy is that the terminal is always displaying the current line. The disadvantage is that examination of text (for example, a command to list lines) may force an extra step, i.e. moving back to the beginning of the text displayed. Clearly there are arguments on both sides. Here again, we believe that the value of the general rule outweighs the merits of a special case. Certainly this issue deserves some thoughtful experiments.

Another typical question in many editors is whether to insert new text before or after the current line. The problem is especially troublesome at the beginning and end of a file. We take the view that the user should be able to do both, as well as be able to insert one or more lines of text in place of the current line. One option is to allow a user to type AFTER, BEFORE, or OVER (AFTER being the default) to the end of an input request. This nicely eliminates the confusion associated with inserting text at the beginning or end of a file, without requiring the user to be aware of an imaginary line located at the end of a file or before the beginning of a file, as is the case in the CMS editor.

One important design detail is the ability to insert short lines of text rapidly. Especially in programs, short lines occur very frequently; for example, simple assignment statements, delimiters (such as *then-else* and *begin-end*) for compound statements and simple procedure calls.

We believe that a user should not be required to enter a special line insertion mode for such cases. Furthermore, users should be able to insert such lines either before, after, or in place of the current line, and to place such lines at the correct indentation without counting (or typing) numerous spaces.

A somewhat similar issue arises during insertion of large blocks of text. The most frequent line inserted by most users is the blank line. Many editors, including CMS, use a line consisting only of a carriage return to terminate input mode. Thus, to create a new blank line, a user must type at least one space on a line. If such a user, quite naturally, presses a carriage return for a new blank line, then input mode is terminated. Some systems treat lines of one blank different from lines of two or more blanks. Each of these alternatives is poor. A user should be able to enter a blank line by simply typing a carriage return, as on an ordinary typewriter. To resolve this problem one solution is to escape from input mode via an interrupt.

We feel that the concept of a margin symbol is also important for easy reference to text at the beginning or end of a line. Nevertheless, there is a rather difficult question about text overlapping lines. For example, should there be two distinct symbols for the margin characters, one for the left margin and one for the right margin? Or should a special end-of-line symbol be introduced? And what about searching for text without regard to line boundaries? One solution is to adopt a single symbol to denote either the left or right margin. An embedded symbol can be taken to mean that the piece of text overlaps a line. For text replacement requests, a margin symbol in a replacement string must be matched with a corresponding symbol in a search string.

These matters are not resolved but again illustrate the importance of *all* design decisions.

Chapter 3

An Example: The Annotated Assistant

As Sterling [1974] and Holt and Stevenson [1977] have pointed out, human engineering is something that must be integrated into the design process, that is, *it cannot be grafted on later.* Very few systems have been designed with first priority given to human factors. The example described here reflects a conscious attempt to design a computer system in which human considerations had top priority in the design process.

3.1 Design Goals

As part of our general attempt to limit the influence of implementation considerations, at the start we chose to complete the design of every system feature before undertaking any implementation. For a variety of reasons, we undertook the task of developing a standard interactive environment for Pascal programmers, although the use of Pascal is incidental to our design. We were interested in assisting both naive and sophisticated programmers.

The effort was motivated by several concerns:

1. the development of a moderately powerful system that makes users more productive with less effort,

2. the need for a system that stimulates rather than dampens the enthusiasm of potential users,

3. a desire to create a system without the trappings of conventional computer concepts, terminology, and jargon.

4. the need for documentation embodying a light and friendly approach to users.

These goals are easy to talk about, but difficult to realize. After nearly two years' work, we produced a design carefully documented in the form of a User's Guide. This document itself was the result of considerable effort. The final design represents a large number of rewrites, perhaps ten, aimed at making the system more accessible to the user. We consider this document to be an example of our overall concern with the human engineering of the system as a whole.

In this chapter, we present the User's Guide (with one appendix) in annotated form. On the pages that follow, the text of the User's Guide appears on the left page and the annotations on the right. The notes are intended to illuminate the human engineering design considerations and to explain the principles motivating our decisions. These principles are the general subject of this book and are often mentioned in the annotations. Some of these principles are more explicitly developed in Chapter 7 as research hypotheses for interactive systems.

The design described here was frozen in the summer of 1976. Since then we have been engaged in a variety of tasks related to it. Considerable effort has gone into a full formal definition of the Assistant [see Singer 1979]. At present, a complete definition of its interactive behavior is done, and a skeletal definition of its entire semantics, including a definition of the semantics of data manipulation performed by the Assistant's editing requests, has been written. A text editor, Hope, based on the Assistant's editing requests, has been written in Pascal. The stand-alone automatic prettyprinting program (also in Pascal) mentioned in the notes is available from the Pascal User's Group.

In reading this paper, it is important to bear in mind that what we are discussing is the *design*, not the implementation, of a system that we believe will be well within the state of the art. Until an actual implementation has been completed, it remains to be seen whether this is the case.

A number of second thoughts concerning the design of the Assistant have also emerged. Whether we will incorporate these into a Revised User's Guide remains to be seen; but for the sake of completeness, we have included these thoughts in the annotations.

A U S E R ' S   G U I D E

to

T H E   P A S C A L   A S S I S T A N T

Introduction

" <u>assistant</u> ... 1. one who assists or gives aid and support; a helper; ... "

> - Random House Dictionary of the English Language

" <u>automation</u> ... 1. a mechanism that is relatively self-operating; esp. ROBOT 2. a machine or control mechanism designed to follow automatically a predetermined sequence of operations or respond to encoded instructions 3. a creature who acts in a mechanical fashion ... "

> - Webster's New Collegiate Dictionary

<u>The Assistant</u>[1]   This section is your introduction to a little robot we have created called "The PASCAL Assistant." This Assistant can help you create, manipulate, and execute PASCAL programs. Like any creature, natural or artificial, the Assistant has its own ideas about things. Unlike ourselves, however, the Assistant's ideas are fairly fixed, and its intelligence is limited. As with any assistant, your understanding of it will make for a smooth working relationship.[2]

<u>Terminals</u>   The Assistant exists as a collection of computer programs that run on a time-sharing computer. Since you and the Assistant interact solely by means of a teletype or some other interactive terminal, we will at times describe the Assistant's behavior

3.2 Introduction to the Assistant

1. An important part of the human engineering of a system is the physical display and organization of its documents. Throughout the User's Guide we attempt to keep a layout that is both visually appealing and yet can be used for quick reference. Because the User's Guide is short, there is little need for an index. Instead, keywords and key phrases are given in the left margin of the manual. These keywords also give the reader a quick clue about the basic idea being presented. We are indebted to Child, Bertholle, and Beck [1971] for this effective scheme.

Perhaps of most importance, the scale of the manual is small. Of course, this is reflected in the smallness of the design itself. Nevertheless, a great deal of care was exercised in eliminating details that the user should, in fact, find out for himself on the system. This is not to say that we believe the manual is incomplete or misleading; rather, a great effort was made to present the system in as concise a manner as possible.

2. One of the most controversial choices we made was to present the Assistant to the user in a consciously anthropomorphic form. From the beginning we describe the Assistant as a creature, robot-like, with a goal structure, consistent behavioral rules, interactive strategies and deductive capabilities. This idea was motivated by several considerations.

In the course of a terminal session, the user must keep track of a great deal of information. For example, the user must continually be aware of the status of his files, his current level of interaction with the system, the consequences of actions he has already taken, and the actions he may legitimately take next. Furthermore, since the actions he may perform are primitive, he must repeatedly supply redundant information over a long sequence of requests. Finally, he must constantly be on guard against destroying his own work by doing something that might seem innocuous, but results in disaster.

In most cases, the kind of information at issue here is readily available to the system. It was our intent that the Assistant take full advantage of the knowledge available to it, and relieve the user of much of the burden of constantly juggling that knowledge.

When we tried to describe a primitive knowledge-based system in a way that would be simple and nonthreatening to users, the natural step was to deliberately exploit the creature-like view which people inevitably apply to machines anyway.

However, what began as a conceptual model for the documentation quickly acquired a life of its own and repeatedly suggested consistent directions for various aspects of the design. This interaction between the documentation and the design was not limited to the conceptual model of the Assistant. In general, whenever we found a feature or concept difficult to explain clearly, we took this as a signal that the design itself was likely at fault. Whole versions of the editing requests were rejected because we could discover no simple way of explaining them.

We benefited in other ways from this view of the Assistant as a creature. For one thing, we were able to avoid much of the dryness associated with the normal type of

in terms of what the terminal does. Because you may be using
any one of a variety of terminal devices, we can only describe what happens in a general way. For specific details
concerning individual terminals, we refer you to "Appendix 1:
Sign-on Procedures and Terminals."[3]

Goals   The Assistant's aim is to function in a way
                   that will be pleasant and helpful to you.
In this end, the Assistant follows three general strategies:

1. It provides you with continuous
    information about its activity.[4]

2. It makes reasonable assumptions
    about what you want to be done
    when specific details are not
    given.[5]

3. It checks with you before carrying
    out a potentially damaging
    operation.[6]

Interaction   These strategies imply a large amount of
with the   interaction between you and the Assistant,
Assistant   especially when you call on it for the first
                   time. However, you will find that interacting
by means of a terminal can become tedious, particularly if the
terminal is slow or if both you and the Assistant are capable
of working at a much quicker pace. As you become more
familiar with the Assistant, you may direct it to assume
that your interaction is to be more abbreviated, just as you
may at any time direct it to assume certain other things about
your working environment.[7]

Request   Requests are made to the Assistant via the
Language   terminal and are expressed in terms of a
                   "request language." This language is
designed to look very much like English and consists entirely
of imperative statements. Several requests allow you to
exchange information with the Assistant concerning almost

manual. And, as the opening paragraph suggests, we were able to introduce a light touch for the reader, and thus make use of the guide a more pleasant experience.

3. Only one of the three appendices to the User's Guide is presented in this paper. Nevertheless, it is important to note that the complete User's Guide (including all the appendices) comprises a document that contains everything the user has to know about the system. The reader need refer to no other documents. This is consistent with recommendations made by Vandenberg [1967].

4. One of the advantages of an interactive system for users is that interaction can be used to couple the system and the user. Unfortunately, few systems provide more than negative feedback to a user, i.e. error messages. Positive reinforcement in the form of highly specific confirmatory messages or an ongoing "chatter" from the system can simultaneously teach the new user what to expect and reassure the user that what he expects is, in fact, going on. A wide body of evidence in psychological reinforcement theory supports the value of this strategy. A further benefit of this interactive strategy is that it allows the resolution of potential ambiguities that may arise in a request. Accommodating such ambiguities permits more flexibility in the language design, especially regarding abbreviated forms.

5. As Gilb and Weinberg [1977] point out, extensive use of "natural" defaults is inherent in all natural language communication, and such defaults may be explicit or implicit. The Assistant is designed to take advantage of both types.

For example, if a program is to be run and no compiled version of it is handy, the Assistant implicitly assumes that it must first be compiled. Moreover, at any time the user may explicitly direct the Assistant to make explicit assumptions about future requests. Thus, the user does not have to continue to specify file names, line boundaries, or options for request when the system can keep track of these details.

6. The philosophy of "security checking" is not novel, but is also not commonplace, and the extent to which it is used by the Assistant may seem extreme. A frequent example is an attempt to overwrite files. Unless told otherwise, the Assistant will always inform the user that a file is about to be destroyed, ask for confirmation, and thus give the user a chance to think twice before going ahead. Another, less obvious, example is the warning a user receives when a text deletion request threatens to destroy a large part of a file. These security checks are intended to give the user confidence that the system will warn him before doing something disastrous. A skilled user may suppress most of these checks.

7. Ideally, we would like an Assistant that knows what level of detail the user needs and adapts automatically; but such intelligence is beyond the limits of cost effectiveness that we have set. The Assistant is intended to be semi-intelligent, only an anything within the scope of its knowledge.

Behavior   At certain times, the Assistant may be
                          attentive, which means that it is awaiting
a response from you. At other times, the Assistant may be
active, which means that it is trying to satisfy a request
for you. Sometimes before a request is satisfied, the
Assistant discovers that it needs more information from you,
in which case it will ask you what it needs to know.

Attentive   Attentive behavior is always signaled by a
Behavior   prompting message, which consists of two
                          characters typed by the Assistant on the
terminal. The prompting message indicates not only that the
Assistant is awaiting a response from you, but also what type
of response is being asked for.

Active   When you send the Assistant a request, it
Behavior   becomes active and attempts to satisfy your
                          request. It does this in three stages:[8]
        1. Verification - The Assistant deter-
            mines whether or not your request
            makes sense, and makes any necessary
            assumptions that it can when specific
            details are not given.
        2. Performance - If the verification
            stage was completed successfully,
            the Assistant will satisfy your
            request. If the operation requested
            is at all time consuming, the Assis-
            tant may indicate its progress at
            various intervals.
        3. Completion - After your request has
            been satisfied, the Assistant indi-
            cates the final result of its actions
            and again becomes attentive.

incremental step toward a truly intelligent system. What we cannot accomplish with limited intelligence we have tried to accommodate with a user-driven adaptive strategy. In some ways, this is one of the least satisfying approaches that we have employed in the Assistant. Not surprisingly, the complexity of the ASSUME request, our vehicle for adaptation, reflects this.

8. There is a body of psychological evidence, [see for example Thorndike and Rock, 1934] which suggests that people "learn without awareness." One implication of these results is that the users of a computer system will infer underlying principles even if they are unaware of doing so.

The Assistant's behavioral goals are not merely "sugaring," but are accurately reflected in its responses. These goals are intended to help the user make reasonable inferences about what the Assistant will do with a particular request. For example, the first goal, verification, ensures that no request will be executed unless it makes sense semantically. In some cases, this implies that significant static prechecking must be performed. This seems a small price to pay for relieving the user of the burden of correcting damage done by a technically legal but senseless request.

Interrupting   While the Assistant is active, you may inter-
the Assistant   rupt it at any time, causing it to become
                     attentive again.   You interrupt the Assistant
in order to ask it for pertinent information or else to tell it
to discontinue attempting to satisfy a request for you and to
attempt to satisfy a new one.[9]

Error   There are several conditions under which a
Conditions   request cannot be satisfied:
1. if the request cannot be understood
    or is inconsistent with what is
    known,
2. if the Assistant asks you to confirm
    a request and you do not comply, or
3. if the performance of the request
    fails for some reason.

Immediate   When a request cannot be satisfied, the
Error   Assistant will identify the problem and
Correction   become attentive.   If an error is found
                  in the verification stage, no action will
be taken.   At this point, you may easily modify and reissue
your request using a request correction facility.   Alternately,
you may issue an entirely new request.[10]

Files   A file is a named collection of information
             that the Assistant maintains for you.   The
Assistant's primary function is to provide you with a means
of creating, manipulating, and performing various operations
with files.   Most files that you will use will be files of
text, and many of these will be PASCAL programs.   When you
create a file, you give it a name.   From then on, both you and
the Assistant refer to that file by the file's name.[11]

Preserving   Any file that you create during a session with
Files   the Assistant will be kept for the duration

9. Most interactive systems have some form of interrupt, but like other details, the interpretation placed on it is often inconsistent or counter-intuitive. The Assistant's interrupt is like a tap on the shoulder. Following an interruption, the Assistant suspends what it is doing, returns with an explanation about what is going on, and asks the user whether he wishes to continue the task. At this point, the user may reply or request additional information. If the user does request additional information, this request may itself be interrupted, but such interruption simply terminates the request for additional information and returns to the original level of interruption. Again, the user is reminded about his original interruption and is asked what to do. Thus, there is no confusing "stacking" of interrupts as, for example, in APL, [Wiedmann 1974], but interruption is always a possible and meaningful operation. This possibility of interrupting a task and carrying out a dialogue concerning the task is patterned after normal discourse. [See Mann 1975 and Palme 1975]. From our view, it is one of the cleanest features to emerge in our design.

10. A fundamental premise in the Assistant's design is that users will make errors. Many interactive systems have facilities for deleting characters or lines as they are being entered. Unfortunately, a user may discover such an error well after it is made. The immediate correction feature is designed to make it simple for users to correct such errors quickly, then with retyping the entire line. If the user makes an error and, as a result, the Assistant discovers that a request is ill-formed, the Assistant will report the error. The user may then change the erroneous line with a conventional edit request, and the Assistant will automatically re-issue the corrected request. While we have never seen this simple feature elsewhere, we believe that it is especially useful for lengthy editing requests and multiple request lines where typing errors are particularly frustrating.

In a similar vein, the UNDO request erases the effect of a request that was performed but did not produce the result desired by the user. The UNDO feature will likely be limited to editing and assume requests, where implementation will not cause severe difficulties.

These are examples of the way the Assistant keeps track of things; in this case, an immediately preceding but unsatisfactory request.

11. While a serious attempt was made in the Assistant's design to avoid the terminology of conventional systems, the concept of a file seems inevitable. In a private correspondence, Hoare suggested the alternative notion of "books" or "folders" supported by an appropriate graphic display. Our decision to support printing terminals ruled this out.

of the session. It may be kept for future
sessions provided that you specifically ask the Assistant to
preserve it for you. No file will be discarded without your
prior approval. Files previously preserved can be modified
at any time. However, at some point the Assistant must be told
whether or not these modifications are to be preserved as well.
Once a modified file has been preserved, its previous condition
is lost forever.[12]

Assumptions   The Assistant retains information about what
                 you have done and what you have explicitly
asked it to assume. Initially, the Assistant uses some basic
assumptions about how you, as a beginner, would want it to
behave.[13] Assumptions, as we've said, enable the Assistant
to reach reasonable conclusions about what you want done when
certain details are omitted from a request. Thus, the use of
assumptions frees you from having to supply excruciating amounts
of detail.

Limitations   As we stated earlier, the Assistant has a
                 very limited understanding. It can make
only very simple deductions based on its restricted knowledge.
When you try to give it a request that it does not understand,
it will tell you so, but it cannot really inform you of the
limits of its own intelligence. This does not mean that its
intelligence is illusory. In fact, you may very well find
its perceptiveness surprising at times.[14]

12. The Assistant uses a simple two-level file system. A good deal of effort went into designing this system so that its operation is largely automatic and transparent to the user. When the user directly refers to a new file, a current temporary copy of it is created. All operations are performed on the current version. At the end of an interactive session, the Assistant asks the user what to do with files that do not have equivalent permanent copies. Although the user must be aware that, potentially, there are two copies of his file, the management of these files is left largely to the Assistant. Specific file manipulation requests enable a user to preserve the current version of a file or restore it to its previously preserved condition.

In retrospect, it is somewhat surprising how much time we spent designing this scheme. Yet, we believe that the concepts of file restoration and preservation in the Assistant are unusually simple.

13. The assumptions for beginners take nothing for granted and attempt to assure that no beginner will be lost too easily.

14. We had reservations about presenting the Assistant as a semi-intelligent creature with moderate self-consciousness that understands a narrow natural language subset. There is always the danger that naive users will come to expect too much and thus be frustrated. We have tried to compensate for this by emphasizing limits, but it may not be sufficient. Nevertheless, we feel that the benefits of an approachable conceptual framework for people are significantly greater than the problems it may create.

Some Notation[15]

<u>Grammatical</u> <u>Notation</u>	Every language has a grammar, and the Assistant's request language is no exception.

Because the Assistant identifies your requests by their form, grammar is especially important in communicating with it. In the descriptions that follow, we employ a special notation to describe the grammatical form of each request.

The rules for this notation are as follows:

<u>Keywords</u>	1. Words shown in upper case are *keywords*. Keywords are like guideposts to the Assistant. They signal what to do and what to expect. Except for PRESERVE, RESTORE, and DESTROY, any keyword may be abbreviated by its first letter. If not abbreviated, a keyword must be spelled out correctly. (See **17.**)
<u>Objects</u>	2. Words shown in lower case and connected with hyphens ("-") are names for the objects of a request that you supply to make the request specific, such as the name of a file, a mode of interaction, or a piece of text.
<u>Alternatives</u>	3. Keywords or objects that are grouped together and separated by slashes ("/") are mutually exclusive alternatives. For **example**:

n/ALL

means that either "n" (a number) or the keyword "ALL" may be specified but not both.

15.   Despite our desire to keep notation and terminology to a minimum, we felt compelled to resort to a kind of context-free grammar. Notations, even simple context-free grammars, can at first be difficult for many users. We attempt a gentle introduction to the use of a few grammatical notations. It is likely that this complexity of the documentation reveals what is probably a weakness in design.

Options 4. Keywords, objects, or any groupings of these that are in parentheses represent parts of a request whose use is optional. For example:

     QUIT (QUICKLY)

means that you may say "QUIT QUICKLY" or simply "QUIT."

Ordering 5. Keywords, objects, or groupings of these may only be specified in the order in which they appear in a rule.

Request Language Summary[16, 17]

General Requests:

EXPLAIN	(name)
SHOW	(name)
ASSUME	assumption
GRIPE	
UNDO	
QUIT	(QUICKLY)

Editing Requests:

NEXT	(lines-of-text)	
PREVIOUS	(lines-of-text)	
LIST	(lines-of-text)	
DELETE	(lines-of-text)	
TRANSFER	(lines-of-text)	INTO file[18]

16.   A major concern in the design was to limit the scale of the Assistant. This was one of the most difficult issues to confront. The tendency to expand and enlarge, to add "powerful" and "important" features was overwhelming. As Miller [1956] pointed out in a stimulating but inconclusive paper, "The Magical Number Seven Plus or Minus Two," there definitely seem to be small limits on our capacity for dealing with large numbers of conceptual objects, but these limits are extended by a phenomenon known as "chunking," in which aggregates can be formed. In spite of the chunking phenomenon, we believe there is a strong intuitive case to be made for keeping things small.

A common criticism voiced over the Assistant's design is that it is a "toy." This was certainly not our intent. However, we have rigorously excluded any feature that we felt would be of use to only a small fraction of users. We believe that the Assistant is an uncommonly simple solution to providing a pleasant and productive working environment for a majority of programmers.

From the request language summary, the small scale and symmetry of the Assistant are immediately apparent. What is not so apparent is the capability that lies with this simplicity. Users of HOPE, our prototype of the Assistant's editing requests, have been surprised by the power of what they took to be a fairly simple-minded editor.

17.   Another major design decision we made was to base the Assistant's request language on a limited English phrase structure. There were a number of reasons for this choice. The natural language of interaction between people is natural language. Even individuals exceptionally experienced with notation have still greater training in natural language. Thus, our aim was to exploit this natural language experience.

Because a reasonable body of experimental data [see, for example, Weist and Dolezal 1972, Epstein and Arlinsky 1965] suggests that people have difficulty in manipulating language-like information that violates normal syntactic structure, we

COPY	(lines-of-text)	INTO file
INSERT	(new-lines-of-text)	(BEFORE/AFTER/OVER)
MAKE	text new-text	

File Requests:

PRESERVE	(file-text)
RESTORE	(file-text)
DESTROY	(file-text)

Program Requests:

RUN	(file-list)	(WITH parameter-file-list)
VERIFY	(file)	(INTO file)
FORMAT	(file)	(INTO file)
BIND	(file-list)	INTO file

General Requests

   The information requests EXPLAIN, SHOW, and ASSUME provide you with the means of exchanging information with the Assistant. You may direct the Assistant to make assumptions about your environment or you may ask it for information about current assumptions, requests, the request grammar, and so on. The use of these requests should make it unnecessary to refer to this User's Guide while interacting with the Assistant.

Explaining Concepts	The EXPLAIN request is your means of getting general information in order to understand something about the Assistant that is not

tried to follow normal syntax as closely as possible and we tried to choose the shortest, most apt, and most orthogonal set of keywords. Short words were chosen not out of typing considerations, but because they occur more frequently and are easier to recall.

While we tried to copy English grammar closely, we did not allow the meaningful reordering of phrases permitted in English, such as "Into A, copy B." We avoided this because of the ambiguities it might introduce into the request language, especially in its abbreviated form. It seems more desirable now to use a more relaxed syntax and resolve ambiguities with an interactive exchange with the user.

Seemingly at odds with the decision to follow natural language syntax strictly was the requirement that the request language have an effective abbreviated form. The ideal, of course, would be to have special function keys for each word, but the real world of ordinary terminals precludes that.

The solution was to introduce the uniform abbreviation rule that *any* keyword can be abbreviated by its *first* letter. Furthermore, abbreviated keyword sequences can be typed *without* intervening spaces. These two rules result in an abbreviated form of requests that is fast and easy to type. Because the rule is so simple, the user can think in the long form while typing its abbreviation. (Because of their potential danger to the user, the three file requests were excluded from this general rule and cannot be abbreviated. This now seems paradoxically inconsistent.)

A variety of data suggests the first letter abbreviation rule. A paper by Freedman and Landauer [1966] points to the usefulness of the initial letter as a recall clue.

This approach to abbreviations is not a "minor" issue. One of the least thought out philosophies of almost every system we have seen is its abbreviation strategy. Abbreviations, like other so-called "details" of design are often very critical, for such details may be the most frequently encountered features of a system. From the user's point of view, ours is a powerful convention. From a designer's point of view, this convention was almost impossible to live with. On many nights we took a thesaurus to bed.

An argument commonly advanced against our abbreviation rule has been that we could not easily expand the keyword list, i.e. add new requests. In rebuttal, we suggest that such additions would be best accomplished by a complete redesign, if all the interlocking design aspects are to receive the consideration they deserve. Furthermore, as the ASSUME demonstrates, any keywords within a request are free from conflict from keywords within other requests.

18. The TRANSFER and COPY requests are good examples of our attempts to follow a limited English phrase structure. Rather than use conventional notations like "TRANSFER lines-of-text, file," we borrow from natural English phrase structure.

Unfortunately, we were not completely successful in following English grammar. From a grammatical point of view, the MAKE request would be better as "CHANGE text TO new-text." However, this suffers from the defect of requiring two levels of delimiting — the string delimiters that bracket text, and the syntactical delimiter "TO." Of course, all this results from the clash between notation (string delimiters) and natural language, an impossible dilemma.

clear.   In order to ask about something, just say:

EXPLAIN (name)

The "name" you give can be any one of a number of words associated with the request language, error conditions, the Assistant itself, or various concepts behind it, like assumptions
or files.

If you say EXPLAIN omitting any name, the
Assistant will respond by giving you information concerning
the last thing that you have done or that has happened to
you.   Each time you say "EXPLAIN" the Assistant will provide
you with more information concerning the topic at hand.   In
addition to its explanation of the given topic, the Assistant
may refer you to other related topics.

If the Assistant does not have information
on a given name, it will tell you so.   If all its information
is exhausted, the Assistant will, if possible, suggest external sources (consultants, references, etc.) that you might
seek out.[19]

Getting   When you want examples of the request
Examples or   language or specific data concerning files
Specific Data   or your working environment, say:

SHOW (name)[20]

In addition to the normal names of things
you might ask about, there are several words which will
direct the Assistant to show you some special things.   These
are:

TIME   - The current time of day.
ASSUMPTION - All of your current
                assumptions.
FILES   - The names and information
                concerning your currently
                preserved files.

3.3   General Requests

19.   A number of interactive systems now incorporate on-line assistance features [e.g. see Teitelman 1974]. To the best of our knowledge none of these are integrated into the system so as to take advantage of an awareness of what is going on. The idea of an integrated assistance feature follows naturally from the general interactive strategy of the Assistant and, as such, is simply a request from the user for greater amplification.

The benefits of this approach are several. The user can directly get information that in a conventional system would only be available in a reference manual. Furthermore, this information can be specialized to his situation. Finally, this information is provided in the context of an actual circumstance where its teaching value and reinforcement potential is greatest. [See Ferster and Skinner 1957].

20.   The SHOW request is also meant to provide pedagogical examples of the request language. For example, if the user types "SHOW MAKE," the Assistant will give examples of the use of the MAKE request. For both the EXPLAIN and SHOW requests, it is expected that over time more information will be added to the Assistant's knowledge base. Coupled with the GRIPE request, this seems to be a viable approach for improving the Assistant's behavior as our knowledge of what needs explanation expands.

Giving
Assumptions

In order to tell the Assistant to make
specific assumptions about your environment
say:

ASSUME assumption

Assumptions fall into several categories.
You can specify one of two modes of interaction by saying:

ASSUME INTERACTION IS TERSE/LONG[21]

These two modes are interpreted as follows:

TERSE - Gives highly abbreviated messages
or none at all. Intended for the
hotshot user.

LONG - Gives loquacious messages, spelling everything out from A to Z.
Intended for the naive or inexperienced user.

Another category determines the amount of
interaction you want the Assistant to assume regarding security
checks for potentially dangerous operations. You can specify
how much security you want by saying:

ASSUME SECURITY IS CAUTIOUS/RISKY[22]

Other uses of the ASSUME request are given further on.

Complaints,
Comments, and
Suggestions

The Assistant, via EXPLAIN and SHOW, is
designed to help you as much as possible
within its limited knowledge. However,
sometimes this is not enough. You cannot
really tell the Assistant your problems and get any kind of
sympathy or advice from it. You can, however, tell the people
in charge your problems through the Assistant by saying:

GRIPE

The Assistant will then go into a special attentive mode where
you may type in a message of any number of lines. You leave
this special mode of interaction by interrupting the Assistant
and making a new request. The text you type will be stored,

21.   Our original design was based on three modes of interaction: TERSE, MODERATE, and LONG. We are grateful to Hoare for pointing out that with a good implementation of the EXPLAIN request two modes should be sufficient.

22.   As Gilb and Weinberg [1977] observe, at times and for some users, automatic protection and forced interaction may be a nuisance.

and at regular intervals all the messages sent by you and others will be sifted out and examined by the people responsible for maintaining the Assistant.[23]

| One Last Chance | If you make a request and you wish you hadn't, you may undo the effect of that request by saying: |

> UNDO

The effects of the most recent request made are cancelled, and you may then proceed as if nothing had ever happened.

| Leaving the Assistant | In order to dismiss the Assistant say: |

> QUIT (QUICKLY)

Before the Assistant will let you go, it will tell you what files have been created or changed and are still to be preserved, and ask you which of those you wish to keep. Furthermore, it will ask you whether or not you want to preserve any new assumptions that you have given it. Finally, it will make doubly sure that you wish to leave before it will let you go.

If you add "QUICKLY" to the request, it will assume that you have already preserved everything you want to keep and will let you go without any fuss.[24]

23. The importance of long range user feedback in maintaining a system cannot be underestimated. In providing a specific request for this, we emphasize its importance and make spontaneous complaints possible. Furthermore, we can take immediate advantage of the system itself to capture inside information about the current state of affairs, which may help us in interpreting a user's complaint.

24. The QUIT request is a good example of our desire to make reasonable and safe assumptions about the user's behavior and still allow more skilled users to override these assumptions.

Editing Requests

Text editing is a process of creating, maintaining, and updating files of text (such as programs, data files, chain letters, or what have you). The Assistant's editing requests make it possible to insert, delete, and substitute text to change the layout and spacing of text, and even to move blocks of text from one file to another.[25]

Editing text commonly requires that a number of changes be made to a particular file. Rather than repeatedly specifying the file to be edited in each request, the Assistant always assumes you want to edit the currently assumed file. (For an explanation of the "currently assumed file" and how it works, see "File Requests - File Assumptions.")

The Current
Line
In making editing requests, you must always have some means of specifying what it is you want changed. The Assistant always assumes that a request is made relative to a "current line." Initially, the current line is the first line of the file. Thereafter, each request that references specific lines causes the last line referenced to become the new current line.[26]

Specifying
Text
Editing may be performed on whole lines or on pieces of text within a line. Operations on whole lines may be specified by giving the number of lines from the current line or by giving a piece of text which appears on a line. References to pieces of text require a special notation to describe the text. This notation has the form:

=text=

The given "text" is any actual sequence of characters. The symbol "=" represents any special character which is neither a letter, digit, space, or semicolon (";"). This special character is used to "bracket" the actual character sequence.

3.4   Editing Requests

25.   In most systems, editing must take place in a special mode or environment. These systems require users to shift levels. The requirement that editing languages be terse usually conflicts with the large scale of the rest of the system. A special editing environment is the logical, if cumbersome, solution to this problem. Then again, many editors are built as independent subsystems and only later incorporated into the main system.

Various studies [e.g. see Turner 1974, Boies 1974] have shown that editing usually accounts for better than fifty percent of the average interactive system's work. Furthermore, the nature of the program development process often leads a user to switch frequently between editing and other tasks.

For these reasons, we believe that a text editor must be designed to be an *integral* part of an interactive programming environment. Central to this belief is our feeling that a user should have access to all the capabilities of the system while editing and vice versa. The use of the "assumed" or default file together with the small scale of the Assistant enable us to keep a single-level system for all requests. We are grateful to David Stemple for making the strong case for this.

26.   One of the larger and more difficult decisions we made was to orient the editing requests of the Assistant around the concept of a "current line." Some editors are "character based" (that is, the user's position in the file may occur in the middle of a line), and others are page oriented (i.e. the interaction is always in terms of multiple lines of text).

Obviously, the kind of terminals in use and the kind of text to be edited enter into this decision. We made a deliberate design decision to orient the Assistant around moderate speed (10-30 cps), typewriter-based terminals without a graphic display facility, as these are at present the most commonly used. We also concentrated primarily on the problem of editing programs. While we did not rule out the possibility that the editor might be used for ordinary language text, the special problems of editing such text were not addressed. [see Lance Miller 1977.]

It might have been better to design the Assistant for a more advanced type of high speed terminal. Indeed, with a bit more storage, some of the "intelligent" terminals made possible by recent advances in semi-conductor technology seem entirely capable of supporting an Assistant locally. The parallelism of display, cursor facilities, definable function keys, and the fast display rate afforded by such terminals would make possible substantial improvements in the design of the Assistant, particularly with regard to the editing requests and the management of defaults.

Since this character indicates both the beginning and ending of the desired text, it must be a character which does not appear in the text itself.[27]

An example editing session is given at the end of this section.

<u>Moving</u>   To move the current line forward say:
<u>Forward</u>   NEXT (lines-of-text)

There are several ways of describing how many lines of text to advance. The NEXT request has the following variations:

1. NEXT
    The Assistant moves the current line
    forward one line.

2. NEXT n
    The Assistant moves the current line
    forward n (where n is a number) lines.

3. NEXT ALL
    The Assistant moves the current line
    forward to the *last* line in the file.

4. NEXT =text=
    The Assistant moves the current line
    forward to the next line containing
    an occurrence of the specified text.

5. NEXT n =text=
    The Assistant moves the current line
    forward to the "n-th" line containing
    an occurrence of the specified text.[28]

6. NEXT ALL =text=
    The Assistant moves the current line
    forward to the *last* line containing
    an occurrence of the specified text.

In our opinion, most editors based on the "current line" concept suffer from the drawback that the user must mentally keep track of what the current line is. This defect results from an inconsistent strategy with respect to line pointer movement. In the Assistant we have deliberately avoided this possible confusion.

The current line is *always* the last line seen by the user. The advantage of this strategy is that the terminal is always displaying the current line. The disadvantage is that the examination of text may force an extra step, i.e. moving back to the beginning of text which is to be displayed. Clearly, there are arguments on both sides. Here again, we believe that the value of the general rule outweighs the merits of a special case. Certainly, this issue deserves some thoughtful experiments.

27. Here again, our use of special notation reveals a weakness of design. We remain dissatisfied with this, but find other alternatives even less attractive.

28. A particularly sticky, but important, detail. Should it be the n-th occurrence or n-th line containing an occurrence? The former seems right for a character-oriented editor, while the latter seems more suited to our line-oriented editor. Endless hours were spent on this issue, with no clear resolution.

In all of the editing requests, "lines-of-text" has the same general form as shown above.[29]

<u>Moving</u> <u>Backward</u>	To move the current line backward say: PREVIOUS (lines-of-text)

The PREVIOUS request is exactly the reverse of the NEXT request. Note that PREVIOUS ALL takes you to the first line in the file.

<u>Displaying</u> <u>Lines</u>	To display one or more lines of text, just say: LIST (lines-of-text)

The variations on the LIST request are similar to the NEXT and PREVIOUS requests:

1. LIST
    Only the current line is displayed
    on the terminal.

2. LIST n/ALL
    The Assistant displays the next n
    (or ALL) lines including the current
    line.

3. LIST n/ALL =text=
    The next n (or ALL) lines containing
    the specified text are displayed.

<u>Deleting</u> <u>Lines</u>	In order to delete one or more lines of text you say: DELETE (lines-of-text)

This operation is virtually identical to the LIST request with the difference that the particular lines specified are not displayed but *removed* from the assumed file.[30]

<u>Moving</u> <u>Lines</u>	To move one or more lines of text out of the assumed file and into another file say: TRANSFER (lines-of-text) INTO file

29. Getting all the editing requests to conform to the same general format for target text patterns was the result of great attention to detail and numerous debates about the proper function of requests. In doing so, we significantly reduced the amount of information a user must learn and remember.

30. An intended security check confirms major deletions with the user.

This request removes the lines of text you specify from the assumed file and puts them into the other file that you name. The lines that are removed will replace the previous contents of the file.[31]

Duplicating Lines	To make a copy of one or more lines of text from the assumed file and place them in another file say:

COPY (lines-of-text) INTO file

This request is exactly like the TRANSFER request except that no lines are removed from the assumed file. Instead, copies of the specified lines of text are placed in the named file.

Inserting Lines	To insert new lines of text into the CURRENTFILE say:

INSERT (new-lines-of-text) (BEFORE/AFTER/
OVER)[32]

The variations on the INSERT request are as follows:

1. INSERT (BEFORE/AFTER/OVER)
   The Assistant will continually prompt you for lines of input from the terminal until you interrupt the Assistant. The lines you type will be inserted before, after, or instead of the current line.[33]

2. INSERT =text= (BEFORE/AFTER/OVER)
   The Assistant will insert the lines specified by text before, after, or instead of the current line.[34]

3. INSERT file (BEFORE/AFTER/OVER)
   The Assistant will insert the contents of the named file before, after, or instead of the current line.

If BEFORE, AFTER, or OVER is not specified, AFTER is assumed.

31. It is not obvious from the User's Guide, but the TRANSFER request is not only intended to excise lines from a file but is the basic mechanism for moving blocks of text within a file. By transferring lines of text to a temporary file, the user can later insert the lines at another point in the file using an INSERT request. This two-step process seemed to offer the user a great sense of security for an operation that on a typewriter-like terminal cannot be visualized very well.

32. A typical question in many text editors is whether to insert new text before or after the current line (or character) position. The problem is especially troublesome at the beginning and end of a file. The Assistant takes the view that the user should be able to do either, as well as to be able to insert one or more lines of text in place of the current line. This eliminates the confusion associated with inserting text at the beginning or end of a file, without requiring the user to be aware of an imaginary line located at the end of a file or before the beginning of a file.

33. The use of the interrupt to terminate continuous text input is consistent with the general semantics of interrupts and allows for easy input of empty (blank) lines, by far the most frequently entered line of text. Empty lines can be entered by simply typing a carriage return.

34. The second form of the INSERT request allows quick insertion of a short text fragment as a line. When combined with the margin symbol, this feature also allows rapid insertion of several short lines of text.

Changing Text   In order to change a piece of text in one
Within a Line   or more lines you say:

MAKE (n/ALL) =text=   =new-text=

This request is different from all the previous requests in that
it operates on text *within* lines rather than whole lines themselves. Starting from the current line, the next n (or ALL)
occurrences of the text given are replaced by the new text given.

If no new text is given between the second
pair of brackets, each occurrence of text will be deleted. The
two bracketing symbols between the text and the new text may be
compressed into a single bracket for brevity's sake.**35**

Editing   Just as all the editing requests depend on the
Assumptions   assumed file for editing, there are other kinds
of assumptions that affect editing. The first
kind of assumption allows you to give special meanings to certain
symbols when you include them in text. These "special-symbols"
can make it easier for you to describe text.

Referring   Sometimes it is useful to refer to text at the
to a Line   left or right margin of a line. To do this
Boundary   you must first define a special symbol to
represent either margin by saying:

ASSUME MARGIN IS special-symbol

If "$" is your margin symbol, then

=$XXX=

refers to a piece of text "XXX" at the beginning of a line,

=YYY$=

refers to a piece of text "YYY" at the end of a line,

=YYY$$XXX=

refers to a piece of text "YYY" at the end of a line followed
by a piece of text "XXX" at the beginning of the next line, and

=ABC=

35. Again, the difficulty of reconciling notation and natural language is apparent.

refers to a piece of text "ABC" that makes up a whole line.[36]
The special symbol consists of one to three
characters. You may select any character provided that it is
not a letter, digit, space, or semi-colon. You may redefine
the margin symbol at any time, or you can say:

ASSUME MARGIN IS NULL

which means that *no* character will be interpreted as a MARGIN.

<u>Using Ellipses</u>   When referencing a long piece of text, it is
tiresome to have to type it all out when only
a few details identify it uniquely. In prose we use three dots
as an ellipsis to indicate that a piece of text has been omitted.
For example, we might quote the previous sentence as: "In
prose, we ... indicate that a piece of text has been omitted."
With the Assistant you may omit pieces of text using a special
ellipsis symbol.
For example, if you have defined "..." as[37]
your ellipsis symbol, then =XXX...YYY= refers to any piece of
text starting with "XXX" and ending with "YYY", and =XXX...
YYY...ZZZ= refers to any piece of text starting with "XXX",
ending with "ZZZ", and having "YYY" somewhere in between. You
define the special ellipsis symbol by saying:

ASSUME ELLIPSIS IS special-symbol

The ellipsis may be redefined at any time, or you can say:

ASSUME ELLIPSIS IS NULL

in which case, no special symbol will be defined as the
ellipsis.

<u>Referring to</u>   Sometimes when referencing existing text,
<u>Character</u>   it is necessary to be able to refer to a
<u>Position</u>   character position rather than a specific
character. For example, suppose you wanted
to find misspellings of the word "pascal." You might want to
refer to something like "p_sc_l", where the underscores ("_")
indicate that any single character is acceptable. You can

36.   We feel that the concept of a margin symbol is important in a program editor, especially for easy reference to text at the beginning or end of a line. Nevertheless, there is a rather difficult question about text overlapping lines.

For example, should there be *two* distinct symbols for the margin characters: one for the left margin and one for the right margin or should a special end-of-line symbol be introduced? And what about searching for text without regard to line boundaries? In the design of the Assistant there is a single symbol to denote either the left or right margin. Two margin symbols are required for text that overlaps lines, and the presence or absence of line boundaries in the pattern must be matched in the text. The matter is far from satisfactorily resolved.

37.   A small but important detail in the human engineering of the Assistant: The user can actually use the familiar ". . ." to denote an ellipsis.

define a special symbol which has this "wild card" meaning by saying:

ASSUME JOKER IS special-symbol[38]

The joker may be redefined at any time, or you can say:

ASSUME JOKER IS NULL

in which case, no symbol will be defined as the joker.

Assuming The second kind of assumption that affects the
Limits editing requests enables you to limit the range
of all subsequent editing requests. Its form is:

ASSUME UPPERLIMIT/LOWERLIMIT IS
CURRENTLINE/NULL

If CURRENTLINE is specified as the UPPERLIMIT or the LOWERLIMIT, then the current line becomes a boundary that all subsequent editing requests may not cross. If the UPPERLIMIT or LOWERLIMIT is specified as NULL, then that boundary is removed.

Assuming a new limit voids any previous one. Assuming a new CURRENTFILE voids all limits.

38. While the joker can be used in conjunction with the margin character to refer to column positions in a limited way, it is far from being a satisfactory solution. Although this is an important problem in text editing, we did not pursue it very far because its importance seemed limited for programmers.

TEXT EDITING SESSION: The user wishes to edit an existing file
                      (◄ indicates the current line)

--ASSUME CURRENTFILE IS POEM 39
  What am I? ◄
--LIST ALL
  What am I?

  They choose me from my brothers: "That's the
  actual number of lines
  Nicest one," they said,
  Candle in my head;
  And they carved me out a face and put a
  Night was dark and will
  But when they lit the fuse, then I jumped! ◄
--PREVIOUS /actual/
  actual number of lines ◄
--DELETE 1
  Nicest one," they said, ◄
--NEXT 1
  Candle in my head; ◄
--TRANSFER 1 INTO HOLD-FILE
  and they carved me out a face and put a ◄
--INSERT HOLD-FILE AFTER
  Candle in my head; ◄
--ASSUME MARGIN IS $
--ASSUME ELLIPSIS IS ...
--INSERT /$$/
     ◄
--INSERT
++And they set me on the doorstep. Oh, the
++
  And they set me on the doorstep. Oh, the ◄
--NEXT 1
  Night was dark and will ◄
--MAKE /will/wilpqrs/
  Night was dark and wilpqrs ◄
--UNDO
  Night was dark and will ◄
--MAKE /will/wild;/
  Night was dark and wild; ◄
--NEXT 1
  But when they lit the fuse, then I jumped! ◄
--MAKE /fuse...jumped!/candle, then I $$Smiled!$/
  Smiled! ◄
--PREVIOUS ALL
  What am I? ◄
--LIST ALL
  What am I?

  They choose me from my brothers: "That's the
  Nicest one," they said,
  And they carved me out a face and put a
  Candle in my head;

39. We believe that users learning a complex task (for example, a new computer system or a new natural language) are helped by examples. This page of the Assistant's manual gives an example of an entire user dialogue. Although not shown here, the example page was also annotated. We believe that even this example is not really sufficient for proper understanding of the Assistant's editing behavior, and the User's Guide as a whole should probably be more example-based.

```
And they set me on the doorstep. Oh, the
Night was dark and wild;
But when they lit the candle, then I
Smiled! ◄
```
--PRESERVE POEM

Figure 1:   Text Editing Session

File Requests

Preserving   Files are normally preserved only during the
Files   dialogue at the end of your terminal session.
                However, if you are wary of erratic behavior
on the part of the Assistant or do not feel at all confident of
reaching the end of your session, then you may explicitly preserve files at any time by saying:[40]

                    PRESERVE (file-list)

If any of the files named in the file list do not exist or have
not been changed since last preserved, then no action will be
taken. You should either correct the request or enter a new
request. (See "Robot's Rules of Order - Immediate Request
Correction.")

Restoring   If any files that have been previously
Files   preserved are changed in any undesirable
                way, then you always have the recourse to
restore those files to their most recently preserved condition
by simply saying:

                    RESTORE (file-list)

                If any of the files in the file list have not
been previously preserved or if any of them have not been changed

3.5 File and Program Requests

40. PRESERVE also provides the user with a defense against an unreliable environment. However, if a system is subject to frequent crashes and the user must frequently interrupt his dialogue to save his work, the result will be a considerable waste of both the computer's and the user's time. Thus, reliability is also a significant human engineering concern.

since they were last preserved, then none of them are restored, and you should proceed as above to correct or reissue the request.

Destroying   If you no longer wish to keep a preserved
Files   file or if you run out of storage space and
                   must discard some files, then you may com-
pletely and permanently annihilate any file by saying:

DESTROY (file-list)

Beware. Once a file is destroyed, there is no way of getting it back very easily. Spare yourself some agony and make sure that you want a file destroyed before you destroy it.[41]

File   All of the editing requests in the previous
Assumption   section depend on having a "currently as-
                   sumed" file to edit. In order to specify
what file is to be assumed simply say:

ASSUME CURRENT FILE IS file

Except where noted, all other requests use the assumed file if a file is not given explicitly.

File   In order to change the name of the CURRENTFILE,
Renaming   all you have to say is:

ASSUME NEWNAME IS new-file-name

Program Requests

Executing   In order to execute a PASCAL program say:[42]
Programs
                   RUN (file-list) (WITH parameter-file-list)

The "parameter-file-list" is a list of file names that are to be substituted for the formal file parameters in the program header of your PASCAL program. If a file exists in your program header but is omitted from your parameter-file-

41. A secondary protection feature that might make this warning unnecessary would be the automatic archiving (for a time) of every file to be destroyed. This was one of the few instances in which implementation considerations were allowed to restrict the design. The archiving of destroyed files now seems to be a less formidable requirement.

42. The spirit of the RUN request is that it runs a Pascal program. The form that the program is in is irrelevant. If need be, the program will be compiled, but this is transparent to the user unless errors are found. The mechanics of keeping track of source and object versions if they are distinct is managed automatically by the Assistant. Of course, complete control of the computer passes to the user's program and the Assistant disappears. From our point of view, this is bad; but the alternative, incorporating a kernel Assistant into the run-time program, seemed overwhelming. Building a kernel of the Assistant into the PASCAL run-time system now seems inescapable, despite the implementation difficulties.

list, then the file name assumed is that of the formal parameter
in the program header. For example, if your program header is:

PROGRAM DUMMY(FILEI,FILE2,FILE3,FILE4,FILE5);

and you type:

RUN DUMMY WITH XYZ,,ABC,DEF

then your request will be interpreted as:

RUN DUMMY WITH XYZ,FILE2,ABC,DEF,FILE5

If more than one file name is given in the
file list, the first file named is assumed to contain the main
program segment, and all the others to contain external procedures. For further information on the linking of externals to
PASCAL programs, see "Appendix 2: Linking External Procedures
to PASCAL Programs."

If a PASCAL error exists in your program, you
will be told so, and your program will not be executed. To see
a listing of those errors use the VERIFY request described below.

Verifying   In order to get a summary of errors in your
Programs   PASCAL program just say:

VERIFY (file) (INTO file)

Depending on whether you have assumed a TERSE or LONG mode of
interaction, you will get either a brief summary of error
messages, a more detailed summary of errors, or a full listing
of your program with error messages. If "INTO file" is specified, the verification will be put into the file instead of
being displayed at the terminal.[43]

Formatting   In order to format your PASCAL program ac-
Programs   cording to standard prettyprinting conven-
                     tions say:

FORMAT (file) (INTO file)

If "INTO file" is specified, the results of the format will be
put into that file; otherwise, they will be displayed at the
terminal.

43.   Complementary to RUN, the VERIFY request is strictly for checking a program. Object code might be generated but that is the Assistant's business, not the user's.

The FORMAT request takes a text file containing a PASCAL source program and reformats it according to a set of standard spacing conventions. FORMAT in no way affects the logical ordering of the program; it merely rearranges the file into a standard format. The standards have been developed so that the reformatted program is aesthetically appealing, logically structured, and above all, readable.

Extra spaces and extra blank lines found in the text are kept. You may improve the readability of your program even more by adding extra spaces and blank lines beyond those inserted by the Assistant.[44]

For example, if your currentfile looks as follows:

```
TYPE SCALE = (CENTIGRADE, FAHRENHEIT);

FUNCTION CONVERT( (* FROM *) DEGREES: INTEGER;
(* TO *) NEWSCALE: SCALE): INTEGER;
BEGIN IF (NEWSCALE = CENTIGRADE) THEN
CONVERT:=ROUND((9/5*DEGREES) + 32) ELSE
CONVERT:=ROUND(5/9*(DEGREES - 32)) END;
```

and you then type "FORMAT", the reformatted program will be printed at your terminal as follows:

```
TYPE SCALE = (CENTIGRADE, FAHRENHEIT);

FUNCTION CONVERT( (* FROM *) DEGREES: INTEGER;
                  (* TO *) NEWSCALE: SCALE): INTEGER;
BEGIN
    IF (NEWSCALE = CENTIGRADE)
        THEN
            CONVERT := ROUND((9/5*DEGREES) + 32)
        ELSE
            CONVERT := ROUND(5/9*(DEGREES - 32))
END;
```

Binding Programs

There may come a time when you simply won't be modifying a program any further, but executing it very often. For execution efficiency you may bind your program into an execute-only file by saying:

BIND (file-list) INTO file[45]

If there are any PASCAL errors in any of your programs, the programs will not be bound and you will be informed of your

44. The FORMAT request is based on a program that automatically prettyprints PASCAL text. A detailed description of the program appears in [Hueras 1976]. This program contains several features that we believe are unique. For one, the program needs no information from the user other than the file itself. For another, the program handles even program fragments. Our initial feeling was that developing an automatic formatting program was easy. This did not turn out to be the case.

45. A vestigial concession to manual program management strategies. On a high level architecture like the Burroughs B7500 it would be irrelevant. (We may have been shortsighted as it now seems to us that even a conventional loader environment could probably be effectively managed automatically by the Assistant.)

situation.

Robot's Rules of Order

<u>Prompting</u>   1.   Two prompting characters are always printed
<u>Messages</u>   by the Assistant to indicate its attentive-
                        ness. The characters indicate what type of
response is expected from you.

Prompting Characters	*Response Type*
(Note: "Ƀ" signifies a space)	
-- **46**	Requests
++	New-Text Input
//	Caution Checks
?Ƀ	PASCAL Program Input

<u>Information</u>   2.   An information request may be issued
<u>Requests</u>   whenever the Assistant is attentive,
                        regardless of what prompting message has
been given. The only exception is the "?Ƀ" prompt, which is
issued by a PASCAL program, *not* the Assistant.[47]

<u>File Names</u>   3.   File names may be of arbitrary length,
                        but no less than two characters. The
characters that may be used are letters, digits, and the blank
character "-". The first character must be a letter and the
last cannot be the break character.[48]
                        For example:

```
SQUARE-ROOT-PROGRAM
SINE-COSINE-FUNCTION
```

3.6 Details and Summary

46. Another detail. We spent a lot of time trying to choose meaningful and distinctive graphics for these prompting symbols because they will be seen so frequently.

47. Probably our darkest hour.

48. The break character for compound names in natural language is the hyphen. Thus, for the request language we use the hyphen to connect compound names. We believe this convention is easy to use and well-founded.

are legitimate file names, while names such as:

> 3QX   (does not being with a letter)
> A   (contains too few characters)
> H3.I   (contains an illegal character)

are not.

Abbreviations	4.	All words in requests, with the exception

Abbreviations
and Request
Spacing

4. All words in requests, with the exception
    of file names and the request names
    PRESERVE, RESTORE, and DESTROY may be
    abbreviated by their first letter.[49]
Spaces in a request may be omitted, with the exception that
files and file lists must be preceeded and followed by a space.[50]
For example:

> TRANSFER 3 INTO ALPHA
> NEXT 5

may be abbreviated as:

> T3I ALPHA
> N5

Multiple
Requests

5. You may type in more than one request on
    a line any time by separating each request
    by a semicolon (";").[51]

Interaction
Control

6. Each of the words TERSE, LONG, CAUTIOUS,
    or RISKY may be appended to any request on
    a line to temporarily override the current-
ly assumed mode of interaction for the duration of the request.[52]
For example, if you are currently assuming LONG messages but
would rather not see a LONG message for an EXPLAIN request, then
you would type:

> EXPLAIN (name) TERSE

49. There are a number of two-word keywords, like CURRENT-FILE, in the request language. It is certainly not clear how to abbreviate them.

50. The requirement that spaces delimit file-names was intended to eliminate ambiguity. Ambiguity now seems rare enough to be worth tolerating.

51. Allowing multiple requests on a line enables the more experienced user to build compound requests. In an environment with slow reaction time it may give the user more satisfaction to work with longer request lines and adapt to the slower pace. As Palme [1975] and others have pointed out, such adaptation is comparable to the adaptation that takes place in natural human dialogue.

This feature is not novel, but the Assistant's interactive "chatter" during execution of a request line and the immediate request correction facility make it more effective.

52. There is some doubt in our minds as to the value of this.

<u>Immediate</u>
<u>Request</u>
<u>Correction</u>

7. Whenever a request is given and not satisfied due to an error, you may correct the error by modifying the request, rather than retyping it entirely. To do so, simply type:

```
=old-text=new-text=
```

In this case, "new-text" will replace the first occurrence of "old-text" found in the erroneous request, and the Assistant will then automatically attempt to satisfy the request again for you. If old-text is not found in the erroneous request, then nothing is done, but you still have the option of trying to modify the request once more. "=" may be replaced by any character other than a letter, digit, or ";", which is neither in old-text or new-text. It is used simply as a separator and is not considered part of either old-text or new-text.

Appendix   The Assistant at a Glance

General Requests:

```
    EXPLAIN    (name)

    SHOW       (name)

    ASSUME     INTERACTION  IS  TERSE / LONG
               SECURITY     IS  CAUTIOUS / RISKY
               CURRENTFILE  IS  file
               NEWNAME      IS  new-file-name
               MARGIN       IS  special-symbol / NULL
               ELLIPSIS     IS  special-symbol / NULL
               JOKER        IS  special-symbol / NULL
               UPPERLIMIT   IS  CURRENTLINE   / NULL
               LOWERLIMIT   IS  CURRENTLINE   / NULL

    GRIPE

    UNDO

    QUIT       (QUICKLY)
```

Editing Requests:

```
    NEXT       (n/ALL) (=text=)

    PREVIOUS   (n/ALL) (=text=)

    LIST       (n/ALL) (=text=)

    DELETE     (n/ALL) (=text=)

    TRANSFER   (n/ALL) (=text=)   INTO file

    COPY       (n/ALL) (=text=)   INTO file

    INSERT     (=text= / file)   (BEFORE / AFTER / OVER)

    MAKE       (n/ALL)  =text=   =new-text=
```

File Requests:

```
    PRESERVE   (file-list)

    RESTORE    (file-list)

    DESTROY    (file-list)
```

Program Requests:

```
    RUN        (file-list)       (WITH parameter-file-list)

    VERIFY     (file)            (INTO file)
```

```
FORMAT     (file)            (INTO file)

BIND       (file-list)       INTO file
```

Request Modifiers: TERSE / LONG
                              CAUTIOUS / RISKY

Request Correction: =old-text=new-text=

Request Spacing:

    Requests   - Spaces in a request may be omitted, with the exception that files and file-lists must be preceeded and followed by a space.

    File-names   - A file-name must be comprised of at least two characters. Characters that may be used are letters, digits, and the break character ("-"). The first character of a file-name must be a letter, and the last character cannot be a break character.

    File-lists   - A file-list is a list of file-names separated by commas (",").

    Multiple Requests   - More than one request may be typed on a line provided that each request is separated by a semi-colon (";").

Prompting Characters and Response Types:

--	Requests
++	New Text Input
//	Caution Checks
?ƀ	PASCAL Program Input

Conventions:

1. Upper-case letters denote reserved keywords.

2. Lower-case letters denote objects.

3. Parentheses denote optional keywords or objects.

4. A slash ("/") denotes mutually exclusive alternatives.

5. "ƀ" denotes a space.

6. All keywords may be abbreviated by their first letter, except for PRESERVE, RESTORE, and DESTROY.

Chapter 4

Formal Description and Design

As mentioned several times earlier, the details of a design are critical to its success. For specifying details, there is a need for a precise framework within which designers can work. We turn now to this topic.

Over the past years, we have had substantial experience in the area of formal description of software. In [Ledgard 1977 and 1980], attempts were made to develop a readable notation for describing a variety of systems. In [Marcotty et al. 1976] a detailed comparison was made of four different formal description techniques. In [Singer 1979] a formal description of the Pascal Assistant presented earlier was attempted. These efforts have met with some but limited success.

Our purpose in this chapter is to summarize our beliefs about the state of the art in formal description, and to present the reasons why we believe this area is intrinsic to good human engineering of interactive systems.

4.1 Motivation

The earliest languages for computers were defined using natural language; many languages and systems continue to be defined in this manner. But as Steel [1966] observed in the preface to the proceedings of the first IFIP Working Conference on Formal Language Description Languages:

Among the principal difficulties facing the designer and imple-

mentors has been an inability to obtain precise descriptions of the formal language with which they must deal.

In the formal language descriptions mentioned above, Marcotty et al. [1976] point out some of the consequences of not having precise description tools. At the top of the list is:

1. Language designers do not have good tools for careful analysis of their decisions.

Both of these statements are still true today.

As an example, the User's Guide to the Pascal Assistant presented in in the previous chapter, while intended as an adequate description from a user's point of view, is far from being a *complete* description of the interactive language supported by the Assistant. Using the Guide as a basis for an implementation would mean that many detailed design decisions would be made during implementation. As was pointed out earlier, because the details of a design may be encountered most frequently by the users, they can have the greatest impact. Clearly the designer should choose these details, and the design should capture them. Without a means for specifying the complete. design of the language exactly, designers can never see all the implications of their designs, and designs will always be completed during implementation.

Thus far, the most successful efforts at achieving precision and completeness in language design have been based on using one or more formal or semi-formal meta-languages to build a description of the language in question. Despite a substantial amount of work in the area of formal definition and specification languages, very little effort has been directed at the problem of describing interactive languages. Given the precision that formal descriptions have provided for static language designs, it seems reasonable that these methods might bring similar precision to interactive language designs.

Nevertheless, there have been a few attempts to create formal descriptions for interactive systems. Some of the interactive features of APL have been defined in APL [Lathwell and Mezei 1971] and Lisp, of course, can be described in Lisp. Parnas [1969] has suggested the use of a "terminal transition diagram" as a tool for specifying interactive terminal behavior.

More recently, an extended form of BNF augmented with actions [Lawson et. al. 1978] was used to describe part of a simple interactive language for a keyboard and display control panel. In the proceedings of the IFIP Working Conference of Command Languages [1975], several approaches to the formal description of operating system command languages are proposed. Of these, probably the most relevant is that of Niggemann [1975], who presents examples illustrating the use of VDL in the definition of a batch-like command language with responses. Finally, there is the work by Embley [1976] on the formal description of a control construct for describing interactive dialogues in the author language of a computer-aided instruction system.

Although all this work is relevant to the problem of formally describing interactive languages, it represents a surprisingly small amount of attention to what is certainly an important problem. Furthermore, to the best of our knowledge, there is no nontrivial interactive system whose *interactive behavior* is supported by a formal definition.

4.2 Special Problems of Interactive Systems

One of the more obvious indications that static and interactive languages present different definitional problems is that so little has been done to apply existing methods for static languages to interactive ones. But, as we shall try to demonstrate, significant obstacles stand in the way of any attempt to extend static methods to the interactive case.

The difficulties begin when we try to define exactly what the scope of an interactive language should be. For example, is it restricted to the legal messages that a user may issue, or should it also include the responses that may be received? What about responses to illegal messages? What about multi-step interactive dialogues? Is the structure of such interactions part of the language? Then again, consider parallelism in interaction, such as the effect of an attention or interrupt signal. Are the intermediate situations and responses which such interruption may create a part of the language?

There are many ways of looking at interactive languages, but it seems obvious that it is their interactive behavior which distinguishes them from static languages, and this behavior cannot be dismissed as incidental. It seems reasonable that we consider interactive languages not only in terms of their effects on data but also their interaction with the user as well.

Unfortunately, this view of the scope of interactive languages leads to complications when it comes to describing them. For example, some definition schemes for static languages describe only legal statements. In these systems nothing at all is said about illegal texts. Yet, practically all interactive languages provide a response to an illegal request from the user. Clearly, a definition for these languages must go considerably beyond the effects of legal requests.

Definitional concepts like syntax and semantics, which are taken for granted in relation to static languages, are not so clear when interactive behavior is added. What, for example, is the meaning of an interactive dialogue seeking information about the contents of a file? Certainly the response to the user must be part of the meaning. Does this imply that the interaction itself is part of the semantics? Is it even reasonable to try to define interactive behavior in terms of syntax and semantics?

Where static languages are concerned, none of these questions need be asked or answered, and the systems developed for defining them can safely ignore these issues.

Given the preceding discussion, it is apparent that the definitional requirements of static and interactive languages are not the same. Some of the principal differences are as follows:

■ Statements in an interactive language can be generated either by the user or in response to the user and *both* have to be described. In a static language, only the user's own statements need to be characterized.

■ Illegal statements generated by the user of an interactive language usually give rise to legal responses. In a static language, illegal texts can be dismissed as meaningless, and only legal text needs description.

■ The interactive responses are as much a part of the meaning as effects on data are. In static languages, data alone can characterize meaning.

■ In interactive languages one message can legitimately interrupt another. In static languages, the text is fixed sequentially.

These differences present new problems for existing definitional systems. Particularly difficult is the absence of the usual clear separation between syntax and semantics, combined with the need to describe interactive dialogues.

For example, attempts to use productions or production-like schemes to develop a "grammar" for interactive dialogues fail because there seems to be no way of introducing nonlinear features like interrupts or message deletion. It also seems inappropriate that responses be determined by syntactic rules. In reality, most responses in interactive languages are semantically determined. Another difficulty of productions is that they do not naturally lend themselves to describing illegal situations. This defect can be corrected by adding error productions along the lines of Aho and Johnson [1974] or Wirth [1968], but these can easily outnumber the productions for legal constructs.

On the other hand, shifting the description of interactive behavior into the realm of semantics has its own drawbacks. Most of the existing formal systems used for semantic description provide no basic mechanism for sequencing because sequential constraints are usually handled in the syntax description. Systems like denotational semantics and axiomatics are particularly limited in this regard.

By its very nature, interaction is a state sequential process. Of course, all of the systems for semantics are mathematically powerful and can be made to model sequencing, but this does not guarantee that these systems will yield a definition of reasonable size and clarity. Another argument against expressing the interactive behavior semantically is the potential confusion that may arise from mixing the interactive behavior with the actual data semantics. A separation between the two seems desirable for clarity's sake.

Most of the existing schemes for definition of static languages benefit greatly from the separation of language features into syntax and semantics. This separation allows two simpler notations tailored to each task to do the job of a single all-encompassing one. As should be evident by now, it is the lack of such a basis for separation, and the resulting necessity of describing more with less, that makes direct application of any of the existing schemes difficult. But is there a different basis for separating the features of interactive languages?

Given the nature of interactive systems, the obvious question to ask is this:

> Does separating the definition of interactive behavior from data
> semantics simplify the definition?

Just as syntax and semantics form the natural components of static languages, perhaps interactive behavior and data semantics are the analogous components for interactive languages?

If we concentrate only on the problems of describing interactive behavior, the need for a state sequencing mechanism assumes great importance, because an interactive dialogue is readily viewed as a sequence of states. As machine designers have long been aware, transition diagrams are a natural state sequencing device. As evidence of this, the behavioral structure of most processors is documented by a transition diagram. Furthermore, as Parnas [1969] points out, the states themselves need not deal with detailed events but may be defined so as to abstract the essential behavioral elements. This kind of approach has been explored by Singer [1979].

4.3 The Value of Formal Descriptions

As mentioned in [Marcotty et al. 1976] the following reasons have traditionally been given to justify the use of formal description techniques:

> 1. *Unambiguous definitions.* There is a need to find a single
> source for answers to questions and, in particular, questions about
> the details of a language or system. User manuals and reference
> manuals, almost always written in English, do not serve this

purpose very well.

2. *Manufacturing specifications.* At present, we have no precise mechanisms to serve as manufacturing specifications for use with vendors. It is impossible to make a contract with a vendor and be assured that the product will conform to our expectations.

3. *Standardization efforts.* Standardization efforts have been impeded by lack of an adequate formal notation. While it is true that there are larger, nontechnical considerations in developing standards, the lack of suitable formal notations is certainly a major obstacle.

4. *Study of languages.* There is a need to study the implications of language design decisions carefully. It is claimed that with a common meta-language we can analyze and compare several source languages in terms of a common definition mechanism.

5. *Resolution of detail.* The use of a formal definition mechanism exposes many design decisions. It is claimed that use of formal definition techniques forces one to resolve details that would otherwise be overlooked in an informal specification.

6. *Detection of design flaws.* In writing a formal definiton of a languge or system, many constructs may be difficult to define. It is claimed that with a suitable definition mechanism, the inconsistencies of a system will be more easily detected. This is a somewhat risky claim, for a given notation may be more suitable to one language or system than another.

Each of these reasons points out some of the benefits of a formal definition, and we support them. However, the task of defining a language or system formally is so difficult (at present) that it is unlikely one would resort to a formal definition to resolve one or two of the above problems.

We believe that the major benefit of formal description is as a *basis for the detailed design of computer systems.* It is our contention that writing a formal definition serves system designers and implementors much as the development of an architectural blueprint serves in the design and construction of a building. If precise definitions are developed during the design process, a much deeper understanding of the entire system results. Furthermore, the definition readily points out the difficulties and special cases that must be resolved before implementation. Finally, the definition allows one to develop a view of the entire system, integrating special cases into a coherent whole.

In a sense, the writing of formal specifications is a design tool for programming at the very highest level. It provides a view of the system from which actual implementation can proceed at a much more rapid rate, and most importantly, with a much higher *quality*.

Chapter 5

The Natural Language of Interactive Systems

Up to this point we have dealt with analytic approaches to the problems of Human Engineering in interactive system design. Many of our conclusions have been speculative.

In this chapter we present the results of an experimental test of a specific human engineering hypothesis derived from the type of analysis examined thus far. The experiment is presented in a traditional, formal way that communicates the results but hides the process by which those results were obtained. To give some further insight into how experimental work in human factors evolves, the next chapter gives an historical diary of the experiment detailed here.

5.1 The Hypothesis

We offer the speculation that command languages should employ a structure and notation that is natural and familiar to the user.

The most natural and familiar form of expression is, for most human beings, their natural language. Unfortunately, natural language as a system is too vague and poorly understood to be used as a complete model for interactive computer languages. There is even the possibility that certain aspects of natural language are fundamentally incompatible with the requirements of man-machine interaction. However, none of this argues against the possibility that certain well-understood attributes of users' natural language can provide a useful starting point for human engineering of interactive command languages.

In particular, we propose the following testable assertion: *an interactive system should be based on familiar, descriptive, everyday words and legitimate English phrases.* This hypothesis is not generally accepted, as evidenced by the vast number of interactive languages that frequently violate it. Our contention is that a system that has these properties will be easier to learn and use than a system that does not have these characteristics but is similar in other respects.

Consider as an example, the following command:

RS: /TOOTH/,/TRUTH/

taken from a typical interactive text editor. RS stands for "Replace String." The effect of the command is to replace the next occurrence of the character string TOOTH with the string TRUTH.

The meaning of this command is not self evident. The syntax is arbitrary in that it does not follow the conventions of any widely used means of communication (widely used in the sense of English phrases or even algebraic equations).

By contrast a command such as:

CHANGE "TOOTH" TO "TRUTH"

(where the individual keywords may be abbreviated according to some convention) is meaningful to any English speaker even without knowing that it is an editing command. The format is that of a legitimate English phrase and the words are both familiar and highly descriptive of the task to be performed. It is clear, for example, that TOOTH is to be changed to TRUTH, and not the other way around. Even the punctuation is based on familiar usage.

To test our hypothesis we chose a simple text editor as the object of our study. Editors are used by a cross section of users ranging from naive to professional. Often, more terminal time is spent editing than performing any other function. Our experiment involved a comparison of two text editors, identical semantically (in terms of editing power) but with differing syntax. One editor was a slightly modified version of the commercially available Control Data Corporation editor supplied with NOS. Its syntax does not resemble that of natural language. The second editor was a remodeled version of the NOS editor, with identical power but with its syntax altered so that its commands were all based on legitimate English phrases composed of common descriptive words.

The experiment was thus both a test of our hypothesis and a demonstration of the effects that human engineering can have on commercially available software in terms of human efficiency, performance, and satisfaction.

A more detailed description of the manner in which this experiment evolved and an annotated diary of its design history are presented in the next chapter.

5.2 The Experiment

Subjects

Twenty-four paid volunteers served as subjects. Equally represented among them were three levels of familiarity with interactive computing.

> *Group 1*, termed "inexperienced users," consisted of eight individuals who claimed little or no experience with computer terminals (less than 10 hours of use).

> *Group 2*, termed "familiar users," was composed of eight individuals who claimed between 11 and 100 hours of experience using a computer terminal.

> *Group 3*, termed "experienced users," consisted of eight subjects who claimed over 100 hours of terminal use.

All subjects were university students of at least average scholastic ability. The inexperienced users were recruited from an introductory computer science course just after they received instruction on the noncomputational mechanics of using a computer terminal but before they received instruction on the use of a terminal as a computational tool. The familiar users had completed the introductory course and were starting their second computer science course. The experienced users had completed several computer science courses and had mastered at least two interactive text editors.

As a requirement for participation, all subjects had to be able to type a presentable college term paper. In addition, none of the subjects had any familiarity with the specific text editors used in the present study.

The Editors

Two text editors were used, termed "the notational editor" and "the English-based editor." The notational editor was modeled after the Control Data Corporation NOS Version I Text Editor. The available commands in the notational editor formed a subset of those found in the NOS editor. The English editor contained the same logical requests but with a syntax dictated by the requirement that all commands be based on legitimate English phrases formed of familiar descriptive words. Table 5.1 summarizes the syntax for the notational editor. Table 5.2 summarizes the revised syntax for the English-based editor.

Procedure

The subjects were informed that the experiment would involve studying text editors and performing some editing tasks. They were told nothing about the rationale motivating the experiment nor about the experimental hypothesis beyond a general statement that the purpose of the experiment was to improve editor design. They were informed of their rights as human subjects in research and were asked to sign a statement of informed consent. Each subject was assigned to either the inexperienced, familiar, or experienced group, depending on the amount of terminal experience.

Each subject was given a manual and table of sample editing commands identical to Table 5.1 or 5.2 except that the editor was not named. Which editor was given was determined randomly for each subject, with the result that one half of the subjects in each experience group received the English-based editor and the other half received the notational editor.

Subjects were free to study these materials for as long as they needed and the experimenter answered any questions. The experimenter then demonstrated the use of the terminal and one editing command. At this point the subject was encouraged to practice using the editor until he or she felt comfortable with it. Practice editing was done using a short list of world gold prices as text.

Following the practice, each subject was given a written copy of some text material adapted from Moody's Industrial Manual. Superimposed on this written copy were a set of proofreader-like marks indicating changes in the text that the subject was to make. The experimenter carefully explained the meaning of these marks. By prior pilot testing, the number of indicated changes in the text was determined to be greater than most individuals could possibly make in the time allotted. This was done to prevent the loss of differential performance information that would have resulted if a number of subjects had accomplished the entire editing task.

Each subject was told that he or she had 20 minutes to make changes and would be scored according to how quickly and accurately the changes were made. The experimenter then allowed the subject to start the task when ready.

Following the completion of 20 minutes of editing, each subject was given the materials for the editor that had not been used previously. Again the subject was allowed to study the materials, ask questions, and practice the commands on the practice text. Then a second text adapted from Moody's Manual was provided, similar in all respects to the first except for the content and required changes. Again each subject was given 20 minutes to perform the

Table 5.1 Summary of Notational Editor

Example Commands	Function
FIND	Current line moves ahead 1 line.
FIND;5	Current line moves ahead 5 lines.
FIND;*	Current line moves ahead to last line in text.
FIND:/TOOTH/	Current lines move ahead to last line in text containing TOOTH.
FIND; -1	Current line moves back 1 line.
FIND; -3	Current line moves back 3 lines.
FIND; -*	Current line moves back to first line in text.
FIND:/TOOTH/; -1	Current line moves back to nearest line containing TOOTH.
LIST	Current line is displayed.
LIST;10	Displays 10 lines starting with current line. New current line becomes last line displayed.
LIST;*	Displays all lines from the current line to the last line of text. Current line becomes last line displayed.
LIST:/KO/;*	Displays all lines with KO that are at or past current line.
DELETE	Erases the current line, next line becomes current line.
DELETE;7	Erases 7 lines starting with current line. Next line becomes current line.
EXTRACT	Puts current line in temporary buffer. Does not change current line.
EXTRACT;8	Puts 8 lines starting with current line in temporary buffer. Current line becomes last line in buffer.
ADD	Computer types two plus signs. Anything typed after is inserted into text after current line. To stop inserting type dual character "Ctrl-T." Current line is then last line you typed.
ADD $	In response to ADD, computer displays two plus signs. Typing "$" inserts contents of buffer into text just after current line. New current line becomes last line from buffer.

Table 5.1 (continued)

CHANGE	Computer erases current line, then types two plus signs. Anything now typed is inserted in place of erased line. Type "Ctrl-T" to stop inserting. Current line is then last line you typed.
CHANGE $	In response to CHANGE, computer types two plus signs. Typing the "$" character erases the current line and replaces it with the buffer. Current line becomes last line from buffer.
RS:/KO/,/OK/	Searches current and all subsequent lines for first KO and changes it to OK. Current line becomes line that was changed.
RS:/KO/,OK/;*	Changes every instance of KO to OK in current and all subsequent lines. Current line becomes last line to be changed.

————————-

IMPORTANT: All commands can be abbreviated to the first letter of each word. It is not necessary to insert spaces between the letters of abbreviated commands. Thus

    LIST:/TOOTH/;*

can be written

    L:/TOOTH/;*

or as

    L : /TOOTH/ ; *

editing task. The entire experimental session occupied about two hours for each subject.

Experimental Design

The experiment employed a mixed analysis of variance design with one repeated-measures variable (consisting of the two editors) and two non-repeated-measures variables (one consisting of the three levels of user experience and the other consisting of the two different orders in which the editors were used). The number of subjects in all of the cells of the design were equal. According to a random assignment scheme, one half of the

Table 5.2 Summary of English Editor

Example Commands	*Function*
FORWARD	Current line moves ahead 1 line.
FORWARD 5 LINES	Current line moves ahead 5 lines.
FORWARD ALL LINES	Current line moves ahead to last line in text.
FORWARD TO "TOOTH"	Current line moves ahead to next line containing TOOTH.
BACKWARD	Current line moves back 1 line.
BACKWARD 5 LINES	Current line moves back 5 lines.
BACKWARD ALL LINES	Current line moves back to first line in text.
BACKWARD TO "TOOTH"	Current line moves back to the nearest line containing TOOTH.
LIST	Current line is displayed.
LIST 10 LINES	Displays 10 lines starting with current line. New current line becomes last line displayed.
LIST ALL LINES	Displays all lines from the current line to the last line of text. Current line becomes last line displayed.
LIST ALL LINES WITH "KO"	Displays all lines with KO that are at or past current line. Current line becomes last line displayed.
DELETE	Erases the current line, next line becomes current line.
DELETE 7 LINES	Erases 7 lines starting with current line. Next line becomes current line.
HOLD	Puts current line in temporary holder. Does not change current line.
HOLD 8 LINES	Puts 8 lines starting with current line in temporary holder. Current line becomes last line in holder.
INSERT TEXT AFTER	Computer types two question marks. Anything typed after is inserted into text after current line. To stop inserting type dual character "Ctrl-T." Current line is then last line you typed.
INSERT TEXT OVER	Computer erases current line, then types two question marks. Anything now typed is inserted in place of erased line. Type "Ctrl-T" to stop inserting. Current line is then last line you typed.

Table 5.2 (continued)

INSERT HOLDER AFTER	Inserts contents of temporary holder into text just after current line. Current line becomes last line from holder.
INSERT HOLDER OVER	Erases current line and replaces it with contents of holder. Current line becomes last line from holder.
CHANGE "KO" TO "OK"	Searches current and all subsequent lines for first KO and changes it to OK. Current line becomes line that was changed.
CHANGE ALL "KO" TO "OK"	Changes every instance of KO to OK in current and all subsequent lines. Current line becomes last line to be changed.

––––––––––

IMPORTANT: All commands can be abbreviated to the first letter of each word. It is not necessary to insert spaces between the letters forming abbreviated commands. Thus

    LIST ALL LINES WITH "TOOTH"

can be written

    L A L W "TOOTH"

or as

    LALW"TOOTH"

subjects in each experience group used the English editor first, while the other half used the notational editor first. Thus although all users used both editors, order of use was counterbalanced and the two orders of presentation were included as an experimental variable.

Testing for Bias

Before the experimental session, each subject was administered a preference questionnaire (shown in Table 5.3) giving three pairs of commands. One member of each pair was modeled after the notational editor and one after the English editor. Subjects were asked to give their preference for one or the other form of commands. A rating of "1" indicated a strong preference for one form of the command, "3" indicated indifference, and "5" showed a strong preference for the corresponding command from the other editor.

Table 5.3   Preference Questionnaire

Below are three pairs of editor commands. Each pair accomplishes the same function even though members of a pair look different. In each case, please indicate which pair member you would prefer to use and how strongly you feel about it using the rating scale beside the commands. Circle the number that best expresses your feelings.

---

1. This pair of commands moves a line pointer back one line.

     Command A: BACKWARD   1. Strongly prefer Command A
                                             2. Mildly prefer Command A
     Command B: FIND; -1   3. No preference
                                             4. Mildly prefer Command B
                                             5. Strongly prefer Command B

2. This pair of commands changes instances of the word TOOTH to TRUTH within a line.

     Command A: CHANGE "TOOTH"   1. Strongly prefer Command A
                 TO "TRUTH"   2. Mildly prefer Command A
                                             3. No preference
     Command B: RS: | TOOTH | , | TRUTH | 4. Mildly prefer Command B
                                             5. Strongly prefer Command B

3. This pair of commands moves a line pointer back to the first line containing the word TOOTH.

     Command A: FIND: | TOOTH | ; -1   1. Strongly prefer Command A
                                             2. Mildly prefer Command A
     Command B: BACKWARD TO "TOOTH"   3. No preference
                                             4. Mildly prefer Command B
                                             5. Strongly prefer Command B

After the session, the subjects were asked to state their preference for the notational versus the English editor, again on a five point scale.

5.3 Quantitative Analysis

The dependent measures taken in the experiment were:

1. The percentage of the editing task completed.
2. The percentage of erroneous commands.
3. A calculation of editing efficiency.

The independent variables were:

1. Type of editor: two levels.
2. Amount of terminal experience: three levels.
3. Order of exposure to the editors: two levels.

The percentage of the editing task completed was calculated as follows. Let

COR   be the number of indicated corrections made to the text
ERR   be the number of erroneous changes made to the text
TOT_COR   be the total number of indicated corrections requested

COMPLETION_RATE = (COR − ERR)/TOT_COR

The percentage of erroneous commands was calculated as follows. Let

SYN   be the number of commands that were syntactically ill-
             formed
SEM   be the number of commands that were semantically
             meaningless
NUM_CMDS   be the total number of commands issued

ERROR_RATE = (SYN + SEM)/NUM_CMDS

The measure of editing efficiency was calculated as follows. Let

POS   be the number of commands resulting in an improvement
             of the text
NEG   be the number of commands resulting in a degradation of
             the text
NUM_CMDS   be the total number of commands issued

EDITING_EFFICIENCY = (POS − NEG)/NUM_CMDS

These measures were hand calculated.

5.4 Results

Table 5.4 summarizes the results of the experiment. Performance figures are given for the percentage of the editing task completed, for the percentage of erroneous commands, and for editing efficiency. For each of these performance measures, means are given for each of the two editors and also for each of the three levels of experience.

All the statements below concerning the statistical significances of results are based upon statistical analyses presented in Table 5.5.

Percentage of Task Completed

Overall the subjects were only able to complete 48% of the editing task using the notational editor as opposed to 63% using the English editor. This difference is statistically significiant at better than the .001 level, which means there is less than one chance in a thousand that this difference is due merely to chance.

Table 5.4 also shows that more of the task was completed using the English editor by each group of users considered separately. There is no statistical basis for concluding that the effects of editor type were different for different levels of experience.

Experience affected the amount of editing work done: the inexperienced subjects, as a group, were only able to complete 35% of the task; whereas the experienced users finished 79%. This effect of experience was statistically significant at the .001 level.

The analysis revealed only one other significant effect: the interaction of task order with editor type at the .01 level. This means that, above and beyond the overall superiority of the English-based editor, users tended to do better on whichever editor they used second.

Erroneous Commands

Disregarding all other factors, the error rate for the English editor was 7.8%, whereas the rate for the notational editor was twice this at 16%. The difference is statistically significant at the .01 level. The data in Table 5.5 suggest that fewer errors were made by more experienced users, but statistical analysis did not substantiate this.

Editing Efficiency

Again the two editors gave rise to significantly different performance, with the English-based editor being used at 51% efficiency, as opposed to 40%

Table 5.4 Summary of Performance Results

(a) *Percentage of Editing Task Completed*

	English Editor	*Notational Editor*	*Average Across Editors*
Inexperienced Users	42%	28%	35%
Familiar Users	63%	43%	53%
Experienced Users	84%	74%	79%
Average Across Users	63%	48%	

(b) *Percentage of Erroneous Commands*

	English Editor	*Notational Editor*	*Average Across Editors*
Inexperienced Users	11%	19%	15%
Familiar Users	6.4%	18%	12%
Experienced Users	5.6%	9.9%	7.8%
Average Across Users	7.8%	16%	

(c) *Editing Efficiency*

	English Editor	*Notational Editor*	*Average Across Editors*
Inexperienced Users	43%	31%	37%
Familiar Users	53%	36%	44%
Experienced Users	58%	53%	55%
Average Across Users	51%	40%	

efficiency for the notational editor. On average, 1.96 commands were required to produce a single editing change using the English editor, whereas 2.51 commands were required using the notational editor.

The more experienced users were able to make more efficient use of both editors. No other experimental factors had a significant effect on editing efficiency.

Table 5.5 More Detailed Statistical Results

The following table gives a detailed summary of the statistical results. It uses the following conventions.

df	This is the number of degrees of freedom.
SS	This is the sum of squares giving the square deviation attributed to source of variance.
MS	This is the mean square deviation.
F	This is the F ratio, the result of a statistical test to determine significance.
**	Indicates that a confidence level better than .01 was obtained.
***	Indicates that a confidence level better than .001 was obtained.

—————————

(a) *Percentage of Editing Task Completed*

Source of Variance	df	SS	MS	F
Total	47	3.041		
Between Subjects	23	2.514		
Task Order	1	.020	.020	« 1
Experience Level	2	1.556	.778	14.962***
Order by Experience Interaction	2	.008	.004	« 1
Error Between Subjects	18	.930	.052	
Within Subjects	24	.527		
Editor Type	1	.226	.226	30.96***
Editor by Order Interaction	1	.082	.082	9.53**
Editor by Experience interaction	2	.023	.012	1.33
Editor by Experience by Order Interaction	2	.001	.0005	« 1
Error Within Subjects	18	.154	.009	

Table 5.5 (continued)

(b) *Percentage of Erroneous Commands*

Source of Variance	df	SS	MS	F.
Total	47	.4198		
Between Subjects	23	.2292		
Task Order	1	.0055	.0055	« 1
Experience Level	2	.0452	.0226	2.3399
Order by Experience Interaction	2	.0033	.0011	
Error Between Subjects	18	.1752	.0097	
Within Subjects	24	.1906		
Editor Type	1	.0739	.0739	13.82**
Editor by Order Interaction	1	.0009	.0009	« 1
Editor by Experience Interaction	2	.0100	.0050	« 1
Editor by Experience by Order Interaction	2	.0096	.0048	« 1
Error Within Subjects	18	.0962	.0053	

(c) *Editing Efficiency*

Source of Variance	df	SS	MS	F
Total	47	1.083		
Between Subjects	23	.680		
Task Order	1	.040	.040	1.90
Experience Level	2	.266	.133	6.49**
Order by Experience Interaction	2	.005	.0025	« 1
Error Between Subjects	18	.369	.021	
Within Subjects	24	.403		
Editor Type	1	.153	.153	14.27**
Editor by Order Interaction	1	.010	.010	« 1
Editor by Experience Interaction	2	.030	.015	1.364
Editor by Experience by Order Interaction	2	.017	.009	« 1
Error Within Subjects	18	.193	.009	« 1

Preference

A measure of which command set the users preferred was taken both before and after using the editors. In the case of the familiar and experienced users, this was done both before and after use; in the case of the inexperienced users, only after use. Table 5.6 shows the results. A score of 1 indicated strong preference for the English commands, 3 no preference, and 5 a strong preference for the notational commands.

All groups clearly preferred the English language editor after exposure to both, but the experienced users showed less of a preference for the notational command set; the experience of using both seems to have caused considerable change of attitude. The experienced group had a slight preference for the English commands prior to editing and changed their preference slightly more in favor of the English commands after completing the editing tasks.

5.5 Implications

The results demonstrate that redesigning the surface syntax of a commercial editor so that the commands more closely resemble English phrases resulted in far better performance. On all measures, performance using the English editor was superior to performance using the notational editor. This was true regardless of the experience level of the users.

Besides being statistically significant, the results are striking in absolute terms. Across all users, the completion rate using the English editor versus the notational editor was a ratio of 63% versus 48% and the editing efficiency at 51% versus 40%. Furthermore, nearly twice as many errors were made with the notational editor. These differences were even sharper among inexperienced and familiar users.

The editors were identical in editing power (semantics) and differed only in the appearance of the actual commands (syntax). In a sense, the English editor is only a variation of the notational; both are basically the same editor. Yet the performance differences were striking. It appears that the surface syntax of a language is quite important from a human engineering point of view.

In the course of running the experiment, the experimenter (Whiteside) was struck by the observation that *the users made no distinction between syntax and semantics.* They simply could not conceive of editing power or function as something different from the appearance of the actual commands. To them, the actual commands embodied the editor to such an extent that many were surprised when told after the experiment that the two editors were functionally identical. This suggests that language designers must be as much

Table 5.6   Results of Preference Questionnaire

	Before Editing	After Editing
Inexperienced Users	——	1.25
Familiar Users	3.25	1.25
Experienced Users	2.75	2.13

– – – – – – – – – –

Key:
1.   Strongly prefer English editor
2.   Mildly prefer English editor
3.   No preference
4.   Mildly prefer notational editor
5.   Strongly prefer notational editor

concerned with surface syntax as with functional features if they hope to design a product to optimize performance.

As mentioned earlier, we were concerned that, since each user was to use both editors, user bias might influence the results. This was the reason for the preference questionnaire. As a whole, the familiar and experienced users showed no bias toward one or the other set of commands prior to using the editors. At the conclusion of the experiment, 22 of the 24 users preferred the English editor. The two subjects who did not were both experienced users. In any event, pre-experimental bias is an unlikely explanation of the results. The users had unlimited time to practice with the editors. This too might produce a bias for one editor over the other. However, the average number of commands issued during practice with the English editor was 14.4 as opposed to 14.7 commands with the notational editor. The difference is not statistically significant and seems so small that different amounts of practice can be ruled out as an explanation of the results.

It is generally accepted that training is more effective with human assistance. As a result, the experimenter was present to answer questions during learning and practice with the editors. We were concerned here too that the experimenter might introduce a bias. To check this, audio tapes were made of the sessions with two subjects; the experimenter was not aware of the actual purpose of the tapes. Here again, we could not detect any bias.

A logical extension of our study would be the examination of asymptotic performance: Would the performance differences remain if users continued to use the editors for a long time? Clearly performance on both editors would improve, and the performance differences would probably decrease. But this would not alter the implications of our result for interactive software design.

First, humans can clearly adapt themselves to difficult systems including ones that have been poorly human engineered. The question is, at what cost? With much practice, people can learn to transmit Morse code at a rate comparable to average two-finger-typing speed, but no one argues that Morse-code senders should replace typewriter keyboards. Why burden users with systems that are difficult to learn when better ones are available?

Second, in our experiment there were performance differences between the two editors even for users with a large amount of interactive computing and editing experience. All the experienced users were well versed with two computer text editors, and most knew at least three. Yet when faced with new editors, they exhibited the same performance differences as individuals who were just learning to use a computer terminal. We feel that the experienced user when faced with a new system or with a system that he or she uses only intermittently is in much the same position as the novice user, and so needs good human engineering just as much.

To test these ideas even further, we performed a small post-experiment study. We recruited four users who had at least 50 hours experience with the notational NOS editor, but no experience with the English editor. With these subjects, no significant performance differences were found, even though the English editor alone was new to these users. We take this small pilot result as again strong confirmation of our hypothesis.

We have shown that a relatively simple change in the syntax of an interactive system results in a much improved product. We believe that this result deserves to have impact on the design of future interactive software systems.

Chapter 6

The Diary of a Human Factors Experiment

The formal mode of presentation used in describing the human engineering experiment in the last chapter tends to conceal the actual process by which the work was done. The design of psychological experiments is always difficult, especially for computer scientists who, naturally enough, are unfamiliar with them.

In this chapter we present an historical diary of the experiment. The diary covers a period of approximately two years. It is presented in the hope of giving some insight of the nature and scope the effort required to perform research in human engineering. Such information is not often exposed.

When this experiment was started, our major concern was not so much the results of testing the given hypothesis, but rather to demonstrate good methodology. In fact, our specific goal was to document our efforts in the form of a diary. Somewhat naively, we thought that by being extremely careful we could illustrate an almost flawless design.

This chapter presents the diary in annotated form. The diary is presented on the following pages, and has been edited to keep its length reasonable. The diary is augmented in two ways. First, the annotations, which are given along side the diary entries. These annotations were made after the entire experiment was concluded and all diary entries had been made. They summarize our main observations about the course of the experiment.

Second, each diary entry is associated with one or more keys, listed as follows:

Advice	Suggestions given by others not directly involved in the experiment.
Alternatives	Design paths and alternatives considered in the design.
Bias	Specific design ideas aimed at developing an unbiased test.
Design	Thinking, analysis, and ideas in the effort to develop an experiment.
Hypothesis	Ramifications and modifications to the original hypothesis.
Implementation	Implementation details faced during the design.
Mistakes	Design decisions for which an initial commitment was made, but later undone.

These keys correspond to a number of major points to be discussed in Chapter 8.

6.1 Early Design Phase

Entries by William Seymour

■ June 7, 1977

I am working this summer as a research assistant for Henry Ledgard. The research, sponsored by a National Science Foundation grant, involves human factors in computer science. I have been reviewing literature in this field and I came across an article that commented critically on the quantity and quality [1.] of actual experimentation. Rarely are proposals for improved human factors design validated by psychological testing, and when the attempt is made, it is usually characterized by sloppy methodology.

■ June 10, 1977   *Hypothesis*

Henry suggests that I do such an experiment as my master's project. He is particularly interested in validating the principle that natural language is the best model for interactive computer languages. We agree this would be the basis of a reasonable experiment and determine to spend a little time each day "brainstorming" the matter.

■ June 17, 1977   *Alternatives, Design*

One method of collecting smaller amounts of data for careful analysis is to collect listings [2.] of actual user sessions and hand check these. One question we could examine would be: Are more errors made using requests that violate natural language syntax? The listings could be collected by scouring the terminal rooms for discarded listings, with rules to assure an appropriately random sample. The most fertile area seems to be the use of text editors: users range from naive to professional and the syntax of the commands involved offers some hope of analysis. After some discussion, Henry and I conclude that adequate control of this type of experiment would be an insurmountable problem. The search goes on.

■ June 20, 1977   *Alternatives*

An investigation of saved system messages also fails to yield any possible experimental data. The only information routinely saved by the system is the log of dayfile messages. [3.] Only syntactically correct commands are saved, making error analysis impossible. No record is kept of text editing sessions or compilations, and the possibility of installing an internal monitor to trap commands is considered too disruptive by the systems people.

■ June 21, 1977   *Implementation, Mistakes*

Repeated dead ends of the sort indicated above have led us to the conclusion that a small scale controlled experiment is the way to go. What we

6.1 Early Design Phase

1. From the outset, we were committed to the design of an experiment of the highest quality. We will see in the entries to follow that we were not always successful. There are so many issues in the design of experiments that it is almost impossible to enumerate them. Some of these issues are: the development of a strong and meaningful hypothesis, the need to expend a minimum number of resources, the use of good experimental materials, and perhaps most importantly, the design ideas needed to ensure that the hypothesis being tested is actually measured. On this last point, we have made most of our mistakes, and strongly believe that this is common in many other experiments as well.

2. This must be one of the most uninspiring and tedious methods for validating any kind of principle. A sound method of experimentation of data collection must aim at one or more, initially stated, specific goals.

3. It seems unfortunate that little work has been done on the routine collection of data that could be used for generalized human factors studies. This is a subject of research in itself.

would ideally like must be constrained by limited resources of time, money, and manpower. We would like a large sample but realize the need for incentive payments must limit us to about one hundred subjects. [**4.**] We would like to observe computer use over time but realize we must make the experiment a "one-shot" proposition.

■ June 23, 1977   *Alternatives, Hypothesis*
We have decided to test the human factors principle: "Natural language provides a suitable model for interactive computer languages." We now must decide how. In our earlier search through discarded terminal listings, we had focused on text editors. This dovetails with Henry's work on the HOPE (Human Oriented Program Editor) system, which is in the final implementation stages. Using the semantics of this system as a basis, we could modify the syntax to our purposes and record subject experience with it. Two experiments are being considered: (a) Design one editor with a mix of "good" and "bad" commands and compare error frequency within subjects. (b) Design a "good" editor and a "bad" editor and compare learning and use results across subjects.

■ June 27, 1977   *Alternatives, Bias, Hypothesis*
We now focus on the natural language principle itself: What is "good" syntax? [**5.**] The HOPE system as designed embodies the principles we want to prove correct, so it seems a reasonable basis for our "good" commands. Generating "bad" commands must be done in a manner to preclude accusations of bias, so we decide to model them on an existing and widely used text editor. We choose the NOS Text Editor. Carrying this idea forward we work on an editor version that has a mix of HOPE and NOS requests and soon hit a snag. If we provide duplicate requests (having different syntax but the same function), the point of the experiment is immediately obvious. If we have only one request for each function, with some functions implemented with "good" syntax and some with "bad," then the error rates observed may be caused by the difficulty of the function rather than the effect of the syntax. For this reason we reject the "mixed" experiment.

■ July 1, 1977   *Bias, Design, Implementation*
We have decided to go with two versions of the editor and an "across-subject" experiment. Henry and I, perhaps belatedly, lay out the following guidelines:
  (a) The editor must be simple enough so that it can be learned fairly quickly.
  (b) The editor must be sufficiently powerful to perform a reasonable editing task and not be just a "toy." [**6.**]
  (c) The semantics of the editor's command language must be

4. Here we see an example of extreme over-optimism. After paying token homage to the need to be cautious about the needed resources, we naively assumed that one hundred subjects was a cautious sample. As the diary continues, we shall see more examples of continued over-optimism about the resources needed for an experiment. This situation is very similar to those encountered in programming, where the scale and difficulties of writing useful programs are notoriously understated at the beginning.

5. It must be true of almost every experiment that the hypothesis itself evolves as the design of the experiment is better understood. Even now, the articulation of our hypothesis is not completely satisfactory. We clearly should have spent considerably more time on the refinement of our hypothesis at the early stages of this experiment. We shall see later that even in the final phases of the experiment, the syntax of the so-called "English" editor had to be redesigned.

6. There is a constant dilemma between the need to devise a simplified controlled situation for an experiment, and the need to be sure that the results thus devised can be extrapolated to a real world environment. In our case, we had to balance the need for a short experimental task against the fact that actual users often perform editing over a period of years. Can we really say that our experimental results would hold over prolonged periods of, albeit intermittent, use? We believe so, but cannot prove it without significantly more testing, and thus, significantly more resources.

This dilemma is typical of almost all experiments. Only careful attention to this concern can hope to alleviate the shortcomings of any experiment.

sufficiently complex to allow the natural language modeled version to demonstrate its presumed superiority over the non-natural language modeled version.

(d) The non-natural language version should not be set up as an obvious "strawman," i.e. no contrived unnaturalness should be installed to ensure its poor performance. [**7.**]

(e) Both versions should be internally consistent and logically complete.

(f) There should be a one-to-one correspondence of functions in the two versions: The two versions should require an approximately equal number of key strokes to execute identical functions.

Our first attempt at the two versions, one like the original HOPE system and one a subset of NOS commands, is not perfect but encouraging.

■ July 12, 1977   *Implementation*

With the first flush of success over, hitting on a viable experiment, comes the sobering realization of how many issues are unresolved. We want the experiment to be as "natural" as possible. Then, if the results bear out our beliefs, we may conclude that the natural language version is superior. This suggests the performance of an editing task rather than the administration of a questionnaire: we want to find out how people react to the editors, not how they perform on quizzes. The rough plan is to train subjects to use the editor by allowing them to study a manual, and then to record their performance on a task. Half the subjects will use one editor version and half the other. Thus committed to a controlled psychological experiment, it seems reasonable to seek advice from a trained psychologist.

■ July 15, 1977   *Advice*

I talk today with Chuck Clifton of the Psychology Department. The conversation is a general one about the process of designing a psychological experiment. His most valuable input is to be consciously aware of all design considerations in order to remove any bias from the experiment.

■ July 18, 1977

What Chuck Clifton said recalled my dissatisfaction with the methodology used in the computer-oriented experiments I have reviewed. I bring this up with Henry and we enthusiastically agree that the *process* of designing a psychological experiment, [**8.**] rather than the experiment itself, would make an excellent project. While we will actually perform a meaningful experiment, the emphasis for my master's project will be on a diary recounting the decisions that went into designing the experiment. We hope that this will prove valuable to other researchers doing similar work.

7. The possibility of bias here is obvious. For our experiment, internal consistency and parallels between the two editors provided an easy trap for invalid comparisons.

For example, when we initially devised the two editors, the syntax was described using a context free grammar similar to BNF. We noticed that the notational editor showed a great deal of consistency as evidenced by the BNF equations. Not wanting to let the English editor fail on this point, we spent a good many hours playing with the syntax of the English editor to make it as internally consistent as the notational editor.

On the other hand, we found it very easy to present the two editors with prose so that the English editor appeared to have a logical consistency not present in the notational editor. The reader who did not see all the commands displayed in a uniform table might thus learn the English editor more rapidly. Continuing problems of this sort were commonplace.

8. It was here that we decided to record our activities in a form of a diary. It was not clear at the outset that the diary would reap many benefits. Now that we have completed the effort, and of course, now that we have had a successful result, the diary seems all that more meaningful. It certainly points out the somewhat chaotic nature of a well-intentioned work.

■ July 21, 1977   *Design, Mistakes*

Since we will be measuring performance effects, we can expect "noise" **[9.]** to be introduced by the different levels of human skill and motivation. These factors must either be explicitly controlled or effectively randomized if we are to have an unbiased result. We could lose any evidence of the effect we seek if any of the following were true:

1. The different editors are too small or insufficiently complex to cause any detectable difference in performance.

2. The performance being measured is too short to yield measurable differences.

3. The sample is too small.

■ July 22, 1977   *Advice*

I am particularly concerned that the effects of the two different syntaxes may be masked by the different skill levels of the subjects. Digging back in my weak and well-atrophied statistical background, I devise elaborate schemes to measure intelligence for use as a covariant. Reason returns and I call the Mathematics Department for help.

■ July 27, 1977   *Advice, Mistakes*

I talked earlier with Ram Dahiya of the UMASS Mathematics and Statistics Department. He listened politely to my covariant designs and carefully shot holes in them. However, he was very optimistic about the chance of finding statistical significance (if the effect is actually there, of course) in a straightforward randomized design. Not completely convinced this was adequate, I next seized the idea of having each subject use first one, then the other editor. I would then combine the total results, factor this to the group mean for total time, and compare differences for the editors within each normalized subject. I raised this possibility with Dan Anderson of the Psychology Department, who pointed out the confounding influence of "learning transfer effects" and the like. He, too, argued for an uncomplicated randomized design, and I now capitulate. **[10.]** With this settled, the statistical work will be relatively simple.

■ July 29, 1977   *Advice, Hypothesis*

I turn my attention next to determining the experimental sample. We wish to test the hypothesis that our English editor is superior but that raises the question: "Superior for whom?" Our sample, we decide, should include a cross-section of people who would be likely to use a text editor. This would include secretaries, students, professional programmers, and researchers. If we recruit randomly, we have no guarantee of getting a suitable mix of user types, and if we recruit by category, our total sample restriction will impose small cell sizes. In the latter case, can we legitimately aggregate results from

9.   Little did we realize the difficulty that we would have on this point. Our primary concerns at this stage in the design of the experiment were: the development of the two editors, the elimination of possible biases, and the implementation problem in following through with the experiment. We tacitly assumed that if we simply followed the ground rules, the result would be there for us to see. Oh, were it so easy.

We consider the presence of noise in an experiment to be one of the most difficult of all problems. This is not a question of proper methodology or proper concern for detail. It is a fundamental question of design itself, which can only be eliminated by thinking, and more thinking.

10.   A fatal mistake. As we shall see later, this decision was finally reversed, even to the point that we allowed a subject to use the second editor immediately after using the first editor. Of interest to us here is the fact that we received the wrong advice. We are sure that in other experiments, the learning transfer effects are so significant that they become a primary issue to avoid. We can only attribute our mistake here to our general unfamiliarity with psychological experiments. We allowed the somewhat cursory advice to overcome our strong intuition on this point.

each subsample to reach an overall conclusion? How small can the cells be and still remain statistically meaningful? Time for another visit to the Statistics Department.

■ August 2, 1977   *Advice*

Ram Dahiya describes a statistical procedure by which results can be normalized for each subgroup, thus allowing aggregation. It is apparently a routine procedure and thus in keeping with my new resolve to hold statistical complexity to a minimum. I am surprised to learn from him that subgroup cells as small as five subjects [11.] will yield analyzable results in many experiments. I double-check this with Dan Anderson, who concurs. I talk with Henry about this and we tentatively agree on four user types: three different levels of computer experience plus one group of subjects with proven secretarial skill. We think this will assure a sample roughly representative of the population of potential editor users. We envision equal cells but haven't yet fixed a total number. That will be largely determined by how much incentive money we can afford, and we don't know yet what we will have to pay [12.] each subject for cooperation.

■ August 4, 1977   *Bias, Implementation*

We will be testing some subjects who have never used a text editor before and who have no computer experience. I am concerned that the presentation of the editor in the manual, no matter how well written, may be too much for some subjects. For this reason, I would like to be allowed to answer questions during the manual familiarization period. This, of course, raises all kinds of biasing problems and will require some thought and advice. A similar question is what happens if a subject accidently deletes the whole file or makes such disastrous errors that he becomes frustrated and quits? The choices then are: (1) assign some maximum time, (2) replace the subject, or (3) throw out this subject. The first solution seems much too arbitrary and the second, considering the recruitment procedure, would seriously contradict our randomization methods, so it appears that we are left with throwing out the subject and having a reduced sample. [13.]

■ August 9, 1977   *Design, Mistakes*

Thus far we have avoided the issue of how to score the results. We want to show that the English editor is "better" in normal use so envision having the subjects first train, then perform an editing task. Henry, Andrew Singer, and I discuss this plan and agree that the most meaningful measurement is the length of time to do the task. Andrew is in favor of keeping track of other details, such as "think" time for the different requests, the ratio of syntactically incorrect requests to correct requests for each type, etc. [14.] I work against the tendency to try to test everything, since this would overly complicate the

11.   For people not accustomed to conducting experiments, the statement that as few as five subject subgroups can provide sufficient data is indeed surprising. There is an intuitive belief that the more subjects, the more meaningful the result.

We argue, as have many others, that the fewer subjects needed to obtain a given confidence level in a statistical result, the stronger the result is. In our experiment, with a total of only 24 subjects, a .001 confidence level was obtained. That, in and of itself, is a strong result.

12.   In a student population such as ours, the money incentive is hard to beat. In our experiment, each subject typically took about two hours and was paid $10 for participation. With this incentive, we had absolutely no trouble recruiting subjects. With the possibility of system failures and the like, in the end we had to recruit about 30 subjects, and thus the total incentive payment was $300. This now seems a tiny price to pay for having ready and willing subjects.

A small aside. We did have problems recruiting, however, but not because of the incentive payment. Initially we developed somewhat elaborate strategies for sign-up sheets, appointments, and the like, well scheduled in advance. This turned out to be a mistake, for many subjects never reported for action. We even resorted to double scheduling, and now have a little more sympathy for the airlines who use this practice. In the end, we opted for on-the-spot recruiting.

13.   We voted for (3). In the end, we actually threw out any catastrophic session, and recruited a new subject. This happened four or five times, mainly due to system crashes.

14.   There is a problem here regarding the collection of auxiliary data. On the one hand, it is nice to collect all kinds of data in order to explore the final result more deeply. On the other hand, the collection and analysis of such data can complicate the running of an experiment.

In the end, we collected a complete listing of every interactive session with the terminal. So far we have made little use of this data. We now believe that such data would be most useful when things go amiss, and this subject will come up again later. Certainly there is *no* substitute for defining the measures to be calculated beforehand, and living with the results of these measures.

experiment. We compromise: the measurements for statistical purposes will include only the time taken to complete the task and the gross number of errors.

■ August 10, 1977 *Mistakes, Advice, Alternatives*
"Normal" use of an editor would presumably be characterized by sporadic use. Thus a "good" editor would have a syntax easily remembered after periods of disuse and we feel our natural language model will have a real advantage here. John Gannon had raised the possibility of recalling subjects after a month for a retest. We do not want to stretch out the experiment that long so we agree on a one-week hiatus and consider what form the retest should be. We would like to have the subjects do another task without permitting reference to the manual. The abort rate for this test, however, would be very high so we decide to give a "closed manual" quiz. Since the subjects have to come back anyway, we decide we might as well train them with the other editor and have them do a second task. The scores on the second task clearly cannot be combined with the first, so will stand as a separate and secondary experiment that will provide results admittedly hard to interpret. [**15.**]

■ August 11, 1977 *Implementation*
The arguments about what information to collect point out one of the biggest lessons I have learned in my conversations with the psychology people: all initial assumptions and all statistical plans must be stated before the experiment is run. The temptation to explain an unexpected result with "free" data is hard to overcome. Thus, although I yield to Andrew's requests to collect any data that may be useful in directing future experiments, I confirm my resolve to apply only preplanned statistical tests to the data designed for these tests. [**16.**]

■ August 15, 1977 *Advice, Mistakes*
Today I talk to Lance Miller and one of his first concerns is the nature of the tasks: Will they be program segments, formatted text, or unstructured character strings. In view of the diverse subjects we will be using, we decide to use text. A book of one page anecdotes by Bennett Cerf proves to be a ready source. These will provide a little interest without being too distracting, a fear that had argued against giving programs to programmers (who might disregard the task and study the code). This still leaves the question of how long to make the text and how many errors to put in. We want the task to take long enough to reflect editor differences but a high density of necessary corrections will be confusing and a long text will penalize those who list the whole file. [**17.**] We realize we will have to wait till the pretest phase to "tune" the tasks to the subject population.

15.   In the end, most of these alternatives were discarded. They were just too complex to implement.

16.   Bravo.

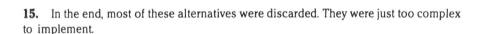

17.   The many little implementation details mentioned here were a continuing problem throughout the design of the experiment. As for the text itself, the anecdotal excerpt from Bennet Cerf proved to be too interesting to the subjects, and thus distracted from the experiment. As far as the other details mentioned, we continued to be overly optimistic about the nature of the editing tasks and the time taken to complete them.

■ August 19, 1977   *Advice*
I talk to Chuck Clifton of the Psychology Department again. One issue we discuss concerns the testing environment: should the test take place in a "natural" environment, for example, in a terminal room where there are other users or in a "laboratory" environment, such as a terminal in a private office would provide. The issue here is a choice between randomization and control. We conclude that using a public room will present too many scheduling problems and opt for the sterile, controlled situation.

6.2   Initial Implementation Phase

■ August 23, 1977   *Advice, Hypothesis*
The experiment is shaping up well but before going to the next level of refinement, Henry and I have lunch with Dan Anderson to discuss the whole project. The chief topic of conversation turns out to be the two syntaxes themselves, and Dan has an interesting question : on what grounds do we claim that our English version reflects natural language? [18.] Since it is true that we did not follow any stated principles in designing the syntax, we will not be able to generalize the result. The criticism is valid but since any attempt to do that now would clearly be post hoc fudging, we can only proceed.

■ August 26, 1977   *Alternatives, Bias*
I return to work on the two versions, enlisting Daryl's help to avoid any implementation snags. One conflict concerns the need to choose keywords for the English editor that will be mnemonically neutral, since we want to test only syntax differences. This is complicated by our desire to retain the first letter abbreviation rule. On this subject we are conservatively modifying an earlier guideline: the two versions only require an equal number of keystrokes if the abbreviation rule is used fully. The notational version will take fewer keystrokes if subjects don't abbreviate and thus we are safe from claims of unfair biasing.

■ August 29, 1977   *Bias*
An important detail is considered today: how honest to be with subjects about the purpose of the experiment. The psychologists advise that the best policy is to be as open as possible within the constraint that full knowledge of experimental purpose could lead opinionated subjects to alter their performance to match their beliefs. We decide to merely state that we are "evaluating two editors." A similar issue concerns the names of the two editor versions. Since materials will be labeled, the names must not indicate our bias. We now choose the neutral initials RS (for revised syntax——the natural language version) and OS (original syntax——the NOS version).

6.2   Initial Implementation Phase

18.   Again, our hypothesis comes under scrutiny. Throughout the experimental design we resisted the scrutiny. We now believe that this questioning of the hypothesis was a critical concern.

■ September 7, 1977   *Design, Implementation, Mistakes*

Not much thought has yet been given to the materials which will be required. The most obvious, of course, are the manuals and the tasks. In addition, the recall quiz will have to be prepared and instruction sheets provided. The manuals are critical: they have to be relatively concise and well-written but must also lend themselves to a perfectly parallel presentation for both versions. **[19.]** I begin work on the manual for the English editor first, using the HOPE manual as a model. The goal is to write it such that the manual for the notational editor can be generated by merely substituting request formats and keywords. Writing and polishing the manuals proves to be very time consuming.

■ September 14, 1977   *Implementation*

As a break from working on the manuals, I develop the other materials. The first is a page of general instructions which introduces each subject to the ground rules and his commitments. In the test session, I will distribute this first then give the appropriate manual to the subject. When the training phase ends, I will hand over detailed instructions for the task, and then finally the test itself and editing requirements. I write the task instructions knowing that they will not be final until Daryl completes the implementation. Henry insists that all materials be coded as text files. If no other purpose is served, I at least get lots of hands-on experience with text editors. **[20.]**

■ September 19, 1977   *Implementation, Mistakes*

A little more thinking about the sample. We earlier decided on four groups: one group with secretarial skill and three with different levels of computer experience. We decide that a typing test will be the arbiter of "secretarial skill" and that "computer experience" will be a function of hours of terminal use claimed. We now decide on 14 subjects per group (or seven per treatment within the group) making a total of 56. These figures have no special statistical significance and represent the best compromise between what we feel is the minimum sample for statistical validity and the maximum we can afford in time and money. **[21.]** As our plans become more elaborate, we must often remind ourselves that the point of this experiment is more to illustrate experimental design than to produce an earthshaking result.

■ October 14, 1977   *Implementation, Mistakes*

A small problem pops up. We have a subgroup labeled "skilled secretarial" for which we will screen to assure a minimum level of typing skill. **[22.]** Should we require no typing skill in other groups and screen it out? This would be a problem since experienced computer users (by our definiition: over 50 hours of terminal use) may test well in typing. We decide to test everyone but only use it as a screening device in the one subgroup. More "free"

19. Underlying all of this concern for the editor manuals was an implicit assumption that the subjects could learn primarily by reading the manuals themselves. We now believe that this was a serious flaw with the initial design of the experiment. We will see later that this was corrected.

In the end, the concern for training subjects efficiently proved to be one of the most important design issues. It is generally accepted that humans learn best when they can ask questions and obtain answers, normally from another person. At this point in our design, we were not completely aware of this point, and later it caused great problems. problems.

20. Although not a result of this experiment, we had a healthy skepticism of too much automation. The merits of storing text on-line are familiar to all of us, and many persons work in an on-line environment almost exclusively. What is often little realized is that there are often (but not always) high overheads associated with the use of a computer. The extra difficulty of inserting text on-line, the time consuming nature of making changes, and the merits of simply using pencil and paper are often ignored. During this experiment we used a computer for which there was limited access: limited in the number of hours during which the computer could be used, and limited in that it required the use of a computer terminal, not always available at our fingertips. In the end, most of the materials were not even maintained on-line; only those materials that were in need of precise maintenance were maintained on-line. We can only say "think before you think you need a computer."

21. Here again we have an example of over-optimism. In retrospect, if we count the time needed to recruit subjects, perform the experimental task outlined in this version of the experiment, and the time to analyze the results, we estimate that at least six hours of effort would be required per subject. Two full months would thus have been required to run the actual experiment. We hardly imagined this commitment of time at this stage of the design.

22. In the final experiment the secretarial group was never used. We had assumed that this group would have special skills that deserved separate analysis. This may be so, but the problem now seems irrelevant to the central purpose of the experiment, and is typical of the kinds of concerns that clear initial thinking should have avoided.

data for Andrew Singer.

■ October 19, 1977   *Implementation, Mistakes*

Daryl reports that the basic HOPE editor is now fully implemented and 98 percent debugged. [**23**] He is thus ready to work on creating the two modified versions for my purposes. I give him the one page summaries of each syntax, and we discuss the other programming requirements that are implied by the task set up. I envision the creation of a procedure that I will call, supplying subject number and editor version. The subject will then be seated at the terminal, will type "START," and the timing will begin. When the file is saved, a checking routine will be activated which will inform the subject that the file matches the goal text or that it does not, display the first nonmatching line, and ask the subject to continue editing. [**24.**]

■ October 21, 1977   *Bias, Implementation*

A problem that has been a nagging worry yields an acceptable solution today. System response time is an unwanted independent variable that is difficult to control. One solution, that of subtracting out system response time from total task time, not only fails to solve the whole problem – user response time is undoubtedly a function of system speed – but also is virtually impossible to implement on the NOS system. If we are able to pair sessions, however, so that a notational subject and an English subject from the same subgroup are tested at about the same time, then this will assure unbiased results. This implies that we must recruit subjects, determine their subgroup, randomly assign them to an editor version, and then recontact them to make an appointment. Complicated but apparently necessary.

■ October 24, 1977   *Implementation, Mistakes*

Daryl has the English version ready for trial. There are only a few bugs and I'm amazed at how quickly it is ready. I recruit a COINS graduate student to try one of the tasks and the results are encouraging. Daryl and I discuss the best way to capture the information we need: as a bare minimum we want the total elapsed time for the task and a count of improperly formed requests. Although they will not be part of the statistical conclusions drawn, counts for each type of request and timings indicating "thought" time are also desirable. The obvious solution is to record all input (user requests) and output (editor responses, including error messages) with the actual time attached to each. [**25.**]

■ October 31, 1977   *Advice, Mistakes*

Andrew Singer and I talk about how I will eventually recruit the subjects. I expect to use all of these methods: [**26.**]

23.   Have you heard that before?

24.   Here we come to a flaw in the attempt to automate the scoring of the experiment. The computer was supposed to compare the edited file with the correct version. A user who inserts an extra blank space at the end of a line, or who does not see some small mistake because the printed version does not clearly highlight the error, may readily be trapped into thinking that the edited version of the file is correct when it is not. Such errors were not germane to the point of our experiment. In the end we went for a simple hand comparison of the user's version of the file with the correct version.

25.   Automatic recording of the entire terminal session was one of the best and simplest ideas for the implementation. Especially when pretesting revealed serious flaws in the experiment, this output was immensely valuable.

26.   Again, unnecessary complexity. There turned out to be no substitute for on the spot recruiting.

(a) Advertise in the UMASS newspaper.
(b) Post notices around the University Computing Center.
(c) Word of mouth and personal recruiting among secretaries in the Graduate Research building.
(d) "Voluntary" recruiting of Introductory FORTRAN students by the teaching assistants.

Since we will be taking subjects at their word about computer experience and non-use of the NOS text editor, questions about these qualifications must be presented in a manner to encourage truthfulness. The incentive payment should be high enough to encourage subjects to return for the second session but not so high as to attract "paid workers."

■ November 18, 1977   *Implementation*
   As the pretest phase approaches, I realize how many small details have yet to be resolved and I practice the sequence of administering the typing test, handing out materials, etc. I arrange the set up of the testing room so that the subject will have a comfortable location and dig up a stop watch to time the typing test and manual reading period.

■ November 21, 1977   *Advice, Design*
   I talk today with Dan Anderson about the possible bias introduced by answering questions during the manual studying phase. We consider and reject as impractical the possibility of hiring someone to administer the test who is unaware of its purpose. The effort of tape recording all sessions also doesn't seem justified. I resolve to wait and let my experience during the pretest determine whether or not questions are allowed.

6.3 Major Difficulties

■ November 28, 1977   *Advice, Design, Mistakes*
   With pretesting almost at hand I call Dan Anderson for advice. He underscores the spirit of the pretesting phase: it is to test the test itself. [**27.**] One of my concerns is whether I can shortcut a few formalities since the first subjects will not be complete strangers to me. Dan suggests that formality is needed only to test the formality itself, and that these results "don't count." I can afford to experiment with different approaches with the first subjects.

■ December 7, 1977   *Implementation*
   I did the first official pretest today with Gwyn Mitchell, a COINS secretary. If I had any doubts about the value of pretesting before, I certainly don't now. One major error showed up. The file I called to be worked on didn't match the file shown in the "Beginning Text" handout.

6.3   Major Difficulties

27.   Throughout the early phases of the design of the experiment we continually misunderstood the value of pretesting. We were under the general misconception that once the experiment was designed, no significant changes could be made to it, and furthermore, that pretesting should be used only for "debugging" the implementation of the experiment. We properly viewed the running of an experiment as a "black box" during which the die is cast and the design cannot be changed. The flaw was that we included pretesting under this black box view.

In fact, pretesting is a powerful aid to the design of experiments. We should have used it much more heavily. We are now aware of several experiments in which the number of subjects that were pretested was even greater than the number of subjects in the actual experiment. Thus, pretesting should be considered as a phase of design, and not simply that of debugging.

Encouragingly, the basic procedures seemed sound and the level of difficulty of the task appeared to be reasonable. A number of small problems reflected my lack of attention to detail and inexperience:

(a) With the terminal in LOCAL Mode for the typing test the carriage return doesn't advance the paper.

(b) With the room set up as it is I must disturb the subject to leave the room.

(c) There is an uncomfortable period while the subject waits as I initiate the task program.

(d) I have no appointment slips for the second session.

After the session I asked Gwyn to comment freely on the experiment. She pointed out a couple of weak spots in the manual but claimed that generally she was able to understand the editing system and the task instructions. Before her session was aborted by our discovery of the wrong starting text, she had appeared to be fluent with the editing requests. We scheduled the second session for a week later.

■ December 8, 1977   *Design*

Last night I repaired the starting text in preparation for the second official pretest. Today's subject was a FORTRAN student recruited from a terminal room. He studied the manual, practiced requests for over an hour, and had worked on the task for almost an hour when he had to leave for a class. Considering that everything else seemed to go smoothly, I was very surprised to have the test take that long. While I suspect that this was an unusually slow subject, it still appears that the task used today is too long. More serious is the great discrepancy in training time: Gwyn studied the manual 18 minutes and did not experiment with any requests. Although Gwyn appeared to have learned better despite this, it seems that allowing unlimited training time may so increase the noise caused by different motivation levels that the experimental effect will be masked. [**28.**]

■ December 13, 1977   *Design*

Abbreviation is rather unpredictably used in the tests for the English editor. Since typing out all the keywords penalizes users in terms of required keystrokes, I ask subjects about this. They confess to a little uncertainty about the universal application of the one-letter abbreviation rule, but also claim that complete spelling is somehow re-enforcing. This is, of course, the sort of effect we are looking for but I still feel it necessary to alter the manuals a bit to underline the abbreviation rule. [**29.**]

■ December 14, 1977   *Design, Implementation*

Gwyn returns after the week's hiatus to do the second session. Since it is so much like the first sessions, all goes well and she completes the task in a

28. Little did we realize the seriousness of this problem.

29. The abbreviation rule was a critical design choice made in order to ensure the rough equality of keystrokes needed for the two editors. When the experiment was later revised and the experimenter illustrated the use of a sample request for each editor, the uncertainty of the subjects over the abbreviation rule simply disappeared.

record time of 16 minutes. I still don't feel the task length is resolved: I'm afraid this last one may be too short to show differences. On the other hand, longer tasks are discouraging to the subject and, if the incentive isn't high enough, they may not return for the second session. Even if they do, the experiment will extend over a six-week period. This is undesirable from the standpoint of maintaining constant motivation (which I expect to fall as students start term work) and system speed (which will also decline as the semester progresses). Two alternatives are to hire another experimenter or to drop the second task. [**30.**]

■ December 21, 1977   *Design*
    Four important issues remain unresolved: the length and complexity of the task; whether to allow unlimited training time; what to do about the second session; and whether to answer questions during training. The first will not be resolved until the final pretesting round and I await advice on the next two. My limited pretesting experience has thus far not helped solve the question problem. Subjects availed themselves of the opportunity to ask me questions very infrequently. Questions asked were of a simple nature. I'm afraid subjects may be embarrassed to display ignorance by questioning me on basic problems. If this continues in the final round of pretesting then I will eliminate question-answering from the actual experiment.

■ December 28, 1977   *Advice*
    I talk with Henry today by phone. We discuss the training time and second session issues and agree to await input from Michael Marcotty, Lance Miller, Andrew Singer, and any psychologists I can buttonhole. These are important decisions and will seriously affect the credibility of the project. Furthermore, in view of our plans to distribute for comment the final version of the proposed experiment before executing it, time is getting close.

■ January 6, 1978   *Advice, Design*
    I talked to Lance Miller briefly this morning. We discussed the training time issue and he took a new approach. He recommended administering a "programmed learning" type training program that would lead the subject through a controlled practice session. [**31.**] In this way, each subject would be assured of a base level of familiarity before starting the task. The time required would be recorded and used as a dependent variable. We agreed to talk again next week.
    Later I talk to Dan Anderson. His views, appropriately, coincide with Chuck Clifton, the other psychologist. Dan is particularly adamant in doing away with the cross-treatment retest. He feels the positive learning transfer caused by the previous experience with the terminal, the task procedure, and editing concepts will interfere with the negative learning transfer of the new

30. Again, here the weaknesses of the experimental design should have been obvious. The continuing tendency to forge ahead obscured the basic problems that were now all around us.

31. The idea of a controlled training session is certainly a good one.

syntax and cause uninterpretable results.

I begin to feel strongly committed [**32.**] to the psychologists' position and prepare my arguments to present to Henry.

■ January 10, 1978   *Design*

I present my case to Henry today. He completes the near consensus and we agree to proceed as follows: the first session of the experiment will remain unchanged except for formally timing the training period. The instructions will be modified slightly to reflect this and to force subjects to make the strategy decision of when to end training and begin the task. The second session will be altered, deleting the second training session and having the second task done using the same editor as in the first task. Reference to the manual will be permitted during the second task but not allowed for the recall quiz which will precede it. In order to keep the total time span of the experiment within reasonable limits I will hire someone to help administer the tests. The last decision brings with it this bonus: we can now schedule the notational and English editors sessions at identical times so that system load variations will have no effect.

■ January 16, 1978   *Implementation*

All the materials are ready. I will do a few more pretests but I expect to make few if any changes. Recruiting will begin in about 10 days and the actual testing should start soon after the students return in February.

Entries by Henry Ledgard

■ April 1978

At this point, Bill Seymour had completed all the agreed requirements for his project. For various reasons, including my participation in France on the DOD Common Language Effort, (the Ada language), the experiment is temporarily halted.

■ December 1978

I have been away for some time. I asked Daryl Winters to pretest a few subjects using Bill Seymour's work. Some subjects never finished the editing tasks, others showed no significant overall performance differences. The detailed listings show some sign of hope, but clearly, something is *definitely* wrong.

■ July 1979

Andrew Singer and I discuss what to do. We need help. He mentions meeting John Whiteside, who has a Ph.D. in Psychology and who has taken an

32.   This issue was constantly annoying us. It was only much later that it was resolved.

interest in this area. Hope reappears, Whiteside is available.

6.4 A Complete Restart

Entries by John Whiteside

■ July 17, 1979   *Design*
   I met today with Henry Ledgard about completing an experiment, evidently started in June, 1977.
   The goal agreed upon was the redesign, [**33.**] completion, and publication of an experiment based upon that described in the earlier entries of this diary. The experiment is to be designed so as to afford the greatest possible chance of finding significant differences in ease of use as a function of editor grammar. At the same time, the highest standards of methodological excellence and freedom from experimental bias are to be observed.
   As indicated in the diary, evidently six pilot subjects were tested. It appears that there was little evidence for differences between the grammars on the basis of overall time to task completion. Henry felt that an effect was present but was being masked by some defect in the experimental design, possibly excessive task length and difficulty.
   As a preliminary estimate, I felt that 2 to 3 months of full time effort would be required to bring the project to fruition. The complete job is to involve the following:
   1.   Bring the experiment to point of being ready for data collection.
   The primary emphasis is the experimental design.
   2.   Keep the diary explaining work done, problems, and decisions taken.
   3.   Maintain close communication with Andrew Singer, especially during the redesign phase.
   4.   Run the experiment.
   5.   Do the statistical analysis.
   6.   Prepare a publication-ready manuscript.

■ July 19, 1979   *Implementation*
   I called Henry and we agreed that my initial responsibility is to bring the experiment into a ready-to-run state within 20 working days. This includes items 1 through 3 above.

■ July 23, 1979   *Design*
   I have become familiar with the experiment and draw up a list of concerns and ideas. The following seem to be the major problems with the

6.4 A Complete Restart

33. At this point we implicitly made a major decision. The entire experiment was put up for inspection, and we prepared to start over. We can only say that the passage of time made this decision much easier to make than it would have been otherwise.

current design: [**34.**]
1.   Experiment too lengthy and cumbersome. [**35.**]
2.   Between-subjects design is not the best choice. Introduces too much variability in a situation where power to detect differences is an overriding consideration. The same subjects should use both editors. Order and practice effects can be handled with pretraining and counter-balancing. [**36.**]
3.   "Natural language" is not spelled out as a model. This may be the experiments most important defect because it makes it impossible to specify exactly what is being tested. I hope to get a better sense of what the designers intended once I can use the editors myself. [**37.**]
4.   Plans for data analysis are primitive and inadequate. We should plan to collect and analyze many variables, not just total time to completion. I agree completely with Andrew Singer's views on this (as represented in this diary). [**38.**]
5.   The "natural language" editor contains a lot of unnatural stuff, for example, line prompts and unusual wordings. The algebraic notation for describing the natural language editor violates the intent of the experiment, I believe. I propose to make the "natural language" editor and the instructions more natural. [**39.**]
6.   I don't believe the post-test is a valid measure since it is so far removed from conditions of actual use. I strongly favor bringing the subjects back for another editing session. [**40.**]
Clearly I need access to the existing pilot data, or else I must generate my own. I also need experience with the editors to get a feel for the experiment.

■ July 30, 1979   *Alternatives, Design*
I continued my review of experimental materials. Ideally I would like to implement a suggestion discarded early on: intermix both types of commands in the same editor. Their objection (confounding of command type with grammar) could be easily met by counter-balancing commands across subjects. The experiment would be simple, quick, and powerful. I suspect though that it may be impractical to implement.

The next best thing would be to simplify the manuals, editors, and texts enough so both can be administered in one session. [**41.**] For one thing, I'm convinced that the materials are much too long and complex as it is, so that most of the variability comes from difficulty in mastering these materials. Secondly, repeated measures is the only way to go, due to the power issue.

I worked on simplifying the editors and the manuals. It appears that a number of the more complex commands can be done away with. So far I have the instructions down to about two-thirds of their original length.

I also formalized alternative experimental designs. All have in common

34.   We make now what is perhaps the most important comment in our diary. In the preceding entries we have seen a great concern for proper experimental methodology. We even go so far as to say that the "methodology" presented earlier was reasonable. Yet, the experiment did not "work"!

With the entry of Whiteside into the scenario, our particular concern was thus not methodology. Instead, it was with *design*: the collection of ideas, thinking, and analysis that is behind any attempt to use proper methodology. It is this concern for the basic premise of an experiment that we believe finally turned the corner on this effort.

35.   Absolutely.

36.   One of the most critical decisions in the redesign of the experiment.

37.   The continuing and nagging problem.

38.   In the end, not much use was made of auxiliary data.

39.   Only another person's eye could see it.

40.   For reasons of complexity, this idea was later discarded.

41.   We made here a large simplification of the experiment. In retrospect, it is surprising how much our experimental materials were littered with concerns that had little to do with the intent of the experiment. We questioned every detail of the materials, with good success.

Another major step in the simplification process was the attempt to administer the entire experiment to a subject in *one* session. While we admit that there are deficiencies in taking this attitude, simplification of the design and execution of the experiment were at this point more critical.

the administration of a practice session followed by exposure to both editors, all in a single session. A follow-up test a week later would involve retesting using both editors.

I called Henry, who will arrange for me to meet with a student whom we may hire to help with the experiment.

■ July 31, 1979   *Design*
I visited Henry to explain ideas so far. He was generally receptive but felt that it was important to discuss certain issues in depth with Andrew, specifically:
> 1.   What should be done with the post-test? Should it be an editing session? Should it be eliminated? What role does it serve in the experiment as a whole?
> 2.   I recommend a repeated-measures design with subjects exposed to both editors during the same session. Are there any problems with such a heavy mixing? [**42.**]
> 3.   To what extent can or should the editors be shortened? Henry and I feel they can be simplified considerably.
> 4.   What data are worthwhile to collect?

Later in the day I met with Richard Scire who answered our notice for programming and systems help. I explained the project to him. He seemed enthusiastic, so I asked him to obtain printouts of Bill Seymour's old files.

■ August 1, 1979   *Design*
I talked further with Rich, whose initial reaction to the experiment was that the natural language editor was not a very good one. It seems he is experienced with and prefers more powerful editors. His comments are interesting in light of subsequent realizations (see entry for August 6, 1979). I am still unable to reach Andrew Singer.

■ August 6, 1979   *Design, Hypothesis*
I reached Andrew Singer and had a lengthy and wide-ranging discussion with him.

The most critical point to emerge is that we cannot proceed with the experiment under the assumption that it will eventually be received by an impartial, objective audience familiar with good psychological research practices. That is, political considerations as well as scientific ones must enter into the design. The audience may be hostile and unreceptive.

This sort of experiment is radical in the eyes of many programmers and systems people. The reason, we agreed (and incidently, the reason that human factors work generally has failed to impact software design) is that the idea of designing an effective man-machine system is in contradiction to the "man versus machine, man competes with machine, man attempts to outsmart

42. The proposal here was to go from one extreme to another. When we had originally considered exposing the subjects to both editors, we felt that a week's hiatus time was an absolute minimum. Whiteside's proposal was to use both editors in the same session.

system" approach common among dedicated computer users. For these individuals, interaction with computers is an end in itself, not a means to an end. The thrill and sense of power in getting the machine to do what you want it to becomes the important source of motivation rather than accomplishment of the task itself.

So we come to the politics [**43.**] of experimental design. On these grounds, Andrew has reservations about the repeated-measures design. Readers may immediately assume that experienced subjects are biased in favor of one or another editor and that this will affect their performance. The between-subjects design is less open to this criticism since the purpose of the experiment will be less obvious to the participants.

I am unconvinced, on grounds of research methodology, that this is a problem, since I believe that most individuals, given proper instructions and incentives, will be motivated to perform well on tasks such as those proposed in this study. But this does not answer the political question.

If we use a between-subjects design, I believe that we enormously reduce our chances of showing anything at all. This is because between-subjects variability, which is always high on complex cognitive tasks, will be especially so given the idiosyncratic and varied approaches that individuals have to editing. All of this variability reduces observed effect in a between-subjects experiment but it is factored out in a repeated-measures design.

My current feeling is to measure biases directly [**44.**] by means of a questionnaire given prior to experience with the editors. (It only makes sense to do this with the experienced subjects).

Since the potential benefits of the repeated-measures design are great, I propose to stick with it at least for pilot testing. I would consider a change in design if pilot testing shows a strong relation between bias and performance.

Another topic of discussion concerns the extent to which the English editor is really a natural language editor. It clearly does not have many natural language features, but it does have common words and phrase structure. I pointed out that this may not be the critical aspect of natural language from the human factors perspective. My guess is that ability to use synonyms and multiple syntactic constructions is more important.

As to the specific issues mentioned under July 31, 1979, Andrew felt that:

1.   The post-test in its present form should be eliminated. If long term retention is an experimental objective then a second editing session should be included. Otherwise, there should be no post-test at all.

2.   We can try the repeated-measures design.

3.   The experiment is too long and cumbersome. However, the editors are probably "minimal" already in terms of what professionals would consider adequate. Further reductions might destroy the credibility of the experiment.

43.   This must be one of the most curious entries in the diary. We had never before considered the "politics" of research in such an explicit manner.

In attempting to do work in human engineering, we have noticed considerable bias on the part of many individuals with whom we have interacted.

In the systems area, there is often considerable bias against work in human engineering. We see two reasons for this bias: (1) there is an implicit assumption in performing human factors work that the systems we have already designed are somewhat flawed. Thus any work is implicitly critical of existing systems.

There also appears to be another, more subtle, bias against this kind of work, that of cost effectiveness. There is a tendency to believe that human engineering improvements results in only superficial gains in performance and use. Thus, human engineering is considered of secondary importance.

Among users, the bias can go both ways. When the subject of human engineering is brought up, many users react with a "go get them" attitude towards the system's designers. Other users are defensive towards any improvement.

44.   In the end, our attempt to measure bias was not particularly conclusive.

4. As many variables as possible should be collected and
analyzed.

Andrew agreed that the algebraic notation should be eliminated from the
manuals. Also, both of us felt that the text was too interesting and that the
required editings seemed arbitrarily chosen. Better to have a more neutral [**45.**]
text and one in which the required changes are repetitious. This will give
subjects a chance to develop stable strategies.

■ August 6, 1979   *Implementation*
I located and restored the original files allowing us to run the original
experiment. Henry and I agreed: (1) to eliminate only a few editor features and
(2) to use the repeated-measures design with a bias questionnaire and (3) to
eliminate the post-test.

■ August 21, 1979   *Implementation*
I finally obtained the pilot data from the original experiment. This
reinforced my conviction that materials were too complex, for the subjects
understood the editors poorly.

■ September 5, 1979
I realized problems with the efficiency measure, and revised it to reflect
not individual commands, but rather the number of successful text changes.
"Editing efficiency" is now defined as the number of successful changes
divided by the total number of commands issued.
I also ran the first pilot subject, with such successful results that we will
start the actual experiment. As for the dependent measures, I will only look at
the percentage of the task completed, the percentage of erroneous commands,
and the editing efficiency.

■ September 13, 1979   *Implementation*
The experiment began today, but problems with system load restrict
running times to early morning and evening hours.

■ October 12, 1979   *Implementation*
Ran last subject today.

■ October 15, 1979   *Design*
Some reflections. The involvement of an experimenter to help the users
learn the editors was essential to the success of the experiment. It made it
possible for the inexperienced users to gain a reasonable knowledge of the
editors in a short period of time. The attempt of the original experimenters to
present the users with only written materials was a mistake — no matter how
well prepared the materials, subjects will misunderstand them and take forever

45.   We finally come to a resolution on the text that should be edited during the experimental sessions. Rather than programs, arbitrary sequences of characters, or "interestng" excerpts from conventional prose, we decide that the text should have some meaning to the user, but the interest in the text should be neutral. In the end, we used a report filed under the Securities and Exchange Commission.

to learn them.

Presenting the editors with a command summary table proved very effective. In fact, almost no one needed to consult the detailed manuals.

Individuals have highly individual strategies of editing, but ones that are consistent for themselves. This means that using a repeated measures design was the right choice; individual variability is just too high to obtain results, unless many, many subjects were run. Editing strategy would make a very interesting future study.

Many of the subjects seemed to feel that only the written changes need be made to the text, that is, that correct spacing and alignment was not important. Again, the repeated-measures design ensures that this variability does not affect the comparison of editors. In scoring, I treated making an indicated substitution separately from getting the spacing in the tables correct.

All of the subjects enjoyed participating in the experiment. Average time per session was one and a half hours. Motivation and interest were high.

Chapter 7

Ten Hypotheses for
Human Engineering Experiments

⊓●━⊓●━⊓●━⊓●━⊓●━⊓●━⊓

These final two chapters discuss future experimental work in human engineering of interactive software. This chapter presents ten human engineering research hypotheses. The hypotheses are summarized in Table 7.1. The chapter following this one presents a non-technical discussion of the design of experiments.

Each of the hypotheses presented here embodies a software design principle that we suspect would contribute to the ease and efficiency of use of any general purpose interactive system. The hypotheses stem from the observation of many users, from basic research in the behavioral sciences, from the literature on human factors in computer systems, and from our own experience. At present, we consider each hypothesis as somewhat tentative.

For each hypothesis a rationale is given. The rationale includes examples, implications for system design, and difficulties as yet unresolved. We also explore ways in which each hypothesis might be subjected to an empirical test.

A number of considerations apply to generating workable experiments from the hypotheses. Among the first considerations are: who will the subjects be and what tasks will they perform. Whichever way these questions are decided, the choices made will limit the generalizability of the experimental findings.

It is important to select subjects from a population similar to that for whom the system is intended. [Ramsey and Atwood 1979] provide a three-category classification of user types: naive, managerial, and scientific or technical; the needs of these users can differ widely. Where resources permit, in any experiment it is wise to include users with at least three levels of experience: inexperienced, highly experienced, and some level of in between.

In testing these hypotheses, an effort must be made either to match individuals on attributes other than experience, to vary such attributes experimentally, or to ensure that assignment of subjects to groups has a random basis. Users differ on many variables: educational level, sex, intelligence, motivation, appearance, and size, to name but a few. One cannot hope to include all of these as experimental variables (the inclusion of two levels of an additional variable doubles the size of an experiment) or even to control all of them. Thus some rule of thumb is needed to decide which variables to include and which to leave out.

In general, a variable should *not* be included in the design unless there is some reason (results of previous research, prediction from theory, or even a hunch) to expect that it will have an important influence on the measures to be taken.

An adequate taxonomy of interactive computing tasks does not exist. If a hypothesis is being tested in the context of a specific application, it will define the experimental task. The hypotheses presented here are phrased in general terms. We assume that text editing is a good first choice for such experiments, since text editors are widely used and the concepts are easily explained to the uninitiated.

7.1 Hypotheses of Scale and Organization

The first three hypotheses deal with the command set considered as a whole rather than with the nature of the individual commands. For example, we believe that users will tend to be overburdened by systems that contain more features than are needed for solving a problem. Such a position has long been accepted in the design of man-machine control systems [see Birmingham and Taylor 1954].

Two of the hypotheses deal with the size of command sets. Many interactive systems include a panorama of commands and features far beyond that required by the typical user. We assert that the smallest possible command set permitting efficient completion of a given task will produce the best user performance. This assertion is supported by the experimental evidence of Baker and Goldstein [1966], who measured user performance with systems containing irrelevant nonsense commands.

Minimizing the number of commands also minimizes the number of alternatives confronting the user. This should have a beneficial effect on performance, as evidenced by results in decision theory [for example, see Edwards 1954].

Table 7.1 Ten Hypotheses

Hypotheses of scale and organization

1. The inclusion of features not needed for a task interferes with task performance.
2. The implementation of features unknown to the user interferes with task performance.
3. Command systems should not be layered or hierarchical.

Hypotheses concerning errors and error correction

4. Error messages should have a positive emotional tone.
5. The user should be alerted to any potentially damaging action.
6. Error correction should be easy and immediate.

Hypotheses concerning command formats

7. Abbreviation rules should be consistent and simple.
8. First-letter abbreviation of command words is a superior abbreviation scheme.
9. Command languages should be based on legitimate English phrases composed of familiar, descriptive words.
10. Commands should be described with examples rather than in generalized form.

It is important to note that in hypothesizing the superiority of small command sets we are *not* making statements about variations in system power. As a very tentative definition, we take "power" to refer to the number of commands required to accomplish a given task. If it is possible to complete a task with fewer commands using a particular command set, that set is more powerful than its alternative. Our hypotheses concerning system size refer to command sets of roughly equal power.

Hypothesis 1: The inclusion of features not needed for a task interferes with task performance.

The essence of this hypothesis is that any system should be pruned to the absolute minimum number of commands necessary to accomplish a given task efficiently.

We contend that many users are intimidated by a system that contains more features than they know how to use. Perhaps these users are tempted to study all the features listed in a manual even though some of them are clearly irrelevant. Of course, some may be tempted to use extra features simply because they are available. This tendency, noted in [Weizenbaum 1976] can cause the user to spend more time mastering subtleties of the system than in attending to the task at hand.

Moreover, an unnecessarily large command set increases the probability of misunderstanding and confusion. As the number of decision alternatives passes a certain level, the efficiency of the human decision maker can deteriorate rapidly [Mann 1977].

Two types of unnecessary features are: (1) extraneous features and (2) redundant features. Extraneous features are those that are clearly unrelated to a task. An example would be a REWIND TAPE command for a user who only edits text in a disk file. Redundant features include duplicate forms of commands and sets of commands that are functionally equivalent. For example, consider a context-oriented editor in which the command:

    CHANGE "TETX" TO "TEXT"

replaces the character string TETX with the string TEXT. Assuming that TETX occurs in column positions 10 to 13, the above command is redundant with the command:

    SET COL 10,13 TO "TEXT"

Elimination of redundant commands does not ensure a command set with the fewest number of commands. The primary source of unnecessary features stems from the basic design ideas and organization of the commands themselves. Two nonredundant command sets, designed to accomplish the same task, can nonetheless contain differing numbers of commands. This point has been discussed in detail in Chapter 2. Our hypothesis argues that it is worth the time and effort necessary to develop the cleanest and simplest set of commands for the given application.

To test this hypothesis, four command sets could be used. One would constitute a minimum set of commands necessary to accomplish a given task. The second set would consist of this minimum set plus a number of redundant commands that duplicated the functions of commands already in the set. The third set would consist again of the minimum set plus additional commands that had no relevance to the task to be performed. The fourth and final command set would consist of commands, greater in number than those in the minimal set, but with no redundant or irrelevant commands.

In designing such a set of commands, care must be taken so that the total number of commands needed to solve the task is roughly equal to that required with the other command sets. Otherwise, the issue under investigation, namely the size of systems, is confounded with another issue, that of the power of individual commands.

The most straightforward design is the separate-users design; that is, the experiment would involve four separate, randomly selected groups of users, each using one of the sets. A same-users design is a possibility but would require careful counterbalancing of order of presentation (there are 24 possible orders). The possibility of complicated order and sequence effects reduces its attractiveness.

How long should the users be allowed to study the command sets prior to testing? Allowing only a fixed time ensures that users will start the task with unequal degrees of understanding of the unequally complicated command sets. A better alternative would be to allow the users unlimited time to achieve some preset level of task proficiency. The study time required would be measured and used as an indication of the difficulty of learning to use the command sets. Once all subjects achieved a given level of task proficiency, further performance differences discovered during testing could be attributed to something other than the users' initial level of understanding.

A major difficulty in testing this hypothesis is that the effects of the extraneous commands will probably vary widely depending upon their perceived interaction with the commands in the minimum set. For example, nonsense commands would probably affect performance less than plausible (but equally extraneous) ones. Resolution of this difficulty would probably involve some pilot testing aimed at identifying the important variables.

Hypothesis 2: The implementation of features unknown to the user interferes with task performance.

Hypothesis 1 deals with system features that are documented parts of a system. The user is aware of their existence and must deduce whether or not they are needed for the task at hand. The current hypothesis deals with features that are *not* known to the user at the outset, but that become evident through use of the system.

The motivation for Hypothesis 2 is our contention that in large systems there are many features that are not known to the user. This is the typical case in systems requiring manuals with hundreds of pages. Examples of such features might include: undocumented commands for which system messages are not self explanatory, limitations on system resources that become apparent only after the user has exceeded them, and system requests for parameters that the user does not understand. In such cases, the user must be concerned with features (when they become apparent) at the expense of concentrating on the problem. As a result, users may become intimidated at the apparent complexity of the system and their own lack of understanding. Alternately, they may become curious and study the extra features, increasing their knowledge of the system, but at the expense of time spent on the task.

This hypothesis and the previous one argue against large scale in systems. But the current hypothesis also argues against the commonly held belief that "subsetting" is an effective remedy to large scale. Unless extraordinary precautions are taken, there is almost no possibility that the user of a kernel or subset of a system can perform a task without, in some way, encountering the larger beast beneath it.

In designing any large system, it is impossible for the designer to know beforehand which features and commands the user will be familiar with. The designer thus implements features with full knowledge of the system. The result is that in practice, system responses will often mystify the user.

In testing this hypothesis we are concerned with demonstrating that the mere presence of unknown features can adversely affect user performance. Clearly, if a system contains more commands than the user is aware of, there is always the possibility that the user will inadvertently activate these with unpredictable results. Although this itself is an argument against large systems, it does not form a part of the present hypothesis.

The hypothesis suggests a number of experiments, each aimed at discovering the effect of a particular class of unknown features. As a preliminary step, a comparison could be made between two systems, identical in all respects except that one gives periodic reports on the status of various aspects of the system that are unknown to the user, whereas the other gives self-explanatory reports. A same-users experiment with counterbalanced order of presentation of the two systems could be used to evaluate user performance.

A second step in the evaluation of this hypothesis might involve requiring the user to respond. For example, one might compare user performance with two systems, one of which periodically asks the user to specify mysterious-sounding parameters (but providing a default option). For example,

```
SPECIFY NEW SYSTEM OVERLAY LEVEL
(N FOR NO CHANGE):
```

The second system would periodically ask for self-evident information, such as:

```
DO YOU WISH TO CONTINUE EDITING?
(Y OR N):
```

As with Hypothesis 1, care must be taken in the selection of the messages used in the two systems. They must differ only in that one type implies the existence of unknown features, while the other does not. Potential for bias exists in selection of the messages as, for example, if the messages pertaining to unknown features were phrased in a threatening way, whereas the other messages were benign. Careful pilot testing with prescreening and rating by judges of messages may be required.

Performance measures called for in these experiments include: amount of work completed in a fixed time, number of errors made, level of user satisfaction with the systems, and some direct measure of the user reaction to the unknown features.

Hypothesis 3:   Command systems should not be layered or hierarchical.

The previous two hypotheses dealt with our concern over the size and scale of interactive systems. The current hypothesis concerns itself with the structure of command sets. By structure we mean a logical organization imposed upon a command set that determines the sequence in which commands may be issued. Our contention is that the structure of command sets may have a profound effect upon user performance.

It is tempting to speculate that systems should simply avoid complexity, but this term has no consistent meaning in the literature. Carlisle [1974] takes complexity to refer to the number of alternative commands that may be issued at any point during an interactive session. He varied the number of alternatives by changing the number of nodes, and a large number of alternatives at each meant high complexity. Carlisle did not obtain consistent performance effects as he varied complexity.

In a related study Whiteside [1979] varied the structure of command sets, a variable that he defined as the degree to which a dialogue grammar imposes syntactic constraints on permissible sequences of commands. Thus a command set in which any command may be issued following any other has no structure, whereas a set in which specific command sequences must be followed rigidly is highly structured. Whiteside demonstrated improved task performance with less structure.

To isolate those organizational variables of command sets that influence user performance, a first step would be to examine the structure found in a number of commercial systems. To avoid some of the difficulties arising from a large command set, quite a number of systems have hierarchical or layered command sets.

As an example, consider the following steps that a user must go through to begin to edit a file. These steps are modeled from a commercial system in widespread use.

First the user must sign on to the system by using the command:

SIGN ON

followed by an account number or password. To use the system editor it is necessary to explicitly call and load it using the command:

RUN EDITOR

At this point, the commands that the system will accept are different from what they were prior to using the RUN EDITOR command. For example, following the sign on, the user is free to call and use any number of programs, including the editor and a file swapping program used for moving files from device to device. However, once the editor has been invoked, calls to these other programs, for example:

RUN FSP

will produce an error message. Notice that logically the system could be designed to allow such a call.

Now assume that the user has loaded the editor. The only allowable options at this point are: (a) explicitly leaving the editor to return to the operating system:

RETURN

or (b) specifying a file to be edited, for example,

IN EXAMPLE-TEXT

In this case, the user is presumably updating a file called EXAMPLE-TEXT.

Notice that at this point the user has descended through several levels of a hierarchy, from the operating system level through the file specification level and now to the level of editing a specific file. In every case, descending to a new level changes the set of commands that can be accepted.

For example, none of the above commands can be issued twice in a row without creating an error message or other difficulty. Thus if the user, having specified EXAMPLE-TEXT as the file to be edited, now wishes to edit PROSE-TEXT instead, it is necessary to issue an explicit command to move back one level in the hierarchy (from the specific file level back to the file specification level):

OUT

Following this, the user can now recall the editor and specify a new file. However, requiring the user to move back a level is not logically necessary.

None of the actual editing commands look like file specification commands; there could be no ambiguity about interpreting file specification commands at the specific file level if the system were designed to do this.

In general, we feel that user performance suffers when systems are layered in this fashion. The user must remember, not just a set of commands, but several sets together with rules for when each set may be used. Further, the user must keep in mind a representation of the hierarchy and what the current level is. All of this amounts to a considerable mental overhead; the user is forced to concentrate on the system and its structure, rather than on the task at hand.

Hypothesis 3 states that layering should be avoided. This means that the system should impose the fewest possible constraints on the permissible orders of command sequences. In the ideal case, the system would accept any command at any time. Obviously the requirements of the task itself may impose logical limitations on the sequence in which commands may be performed. For example, it would make no sense to edit a file prior to specifying the file to be edited. However, the system should not impose its own constraints in addition to those required by the logic of the task to be performed.

The verification of this hypothesis requires creation of two interactive command sets designed to accomplish the same task. They would differ from one another only in that one is hierarchically structured, while the other is not. One of the most difficult aspects of this design is devising two command systems that will allow the task to be performed using the same number of commands; hierarchical command sets tend to require users to issue more commands than their nonhierarchical counterparts.

A hypothesis of this generality should be tested with a variety of tasks. One obvious choice is a task requiring the user to move, swap, and replace a number of files located in a number of simulated storage devices. Performance measures required include: time needed to learn the system, amount of work done in a given time, and number of syntactic errors.

7.2 Hypotheses Concerning Errors and Error Correction

In their literature survey, Ramsey and Atwood [1979] found that the bulk of the literature concerned with user errors deals with data entry and programming errors. They found only a few studies that dealt with interactive dialogue errors and these were aimed at discovering properties of dialogues leading to errors. Our position is that although good system design can reduce error frequency, it can never eliminate errors altogether. Further, although it may be possible to automate error detection and correction for certain simple categories of error, the possibility of doing the same for conceptual errors remains theoretically unproven, much less practically possible.

Given the inevitability of errors, we hypothesize that user performance will be greatly affected by the manner in which the system responds to errors.

Hypothesis 4: *Error messages should have a positive emotional tone.*

Even the most rational individual can become enraged at a tool that does not work properly. Computers present attributes to us that resemble human attributes in many ways. For example, they talk back and tell us that we have made errors. If people can become angry at inanimate objects that bear no resemblance to human beings, surely it is unreasonable to expect them to remain calm when they are actually insulted by a machine! And yet messages such as FATAL ERROR are common.

Even error messages that are not overtly insulting usually carry with them the implication that the user is at fault. Error messages, besides being informative, should be phrased positively and avoid this implication. For example, if the user types something unrecognizable, instead of responding with BAD INPUT STRING, which puts the responsibility squarely on the user, a better message might be UNRECOGNIZED TEXT or even I'M CONFUSED, which implies that the lack of understanding may be a result of the computer's inadequacy rather than the user's carelessness.

Such a hypothesis is relatively straightforward to test. The main difficulty lies in composing several lists of error messages that vary in emotional tone. A useful procedure in such cases is to compose preliminary lists and then ask a panel of judges to rate the items according to the variable of interest. Thus a set of messages could be compiled and a panel of judges asked to sort them into categories of negative, neutral, and positive in emotional tone. Items on which there was general agreement could then be used in the experiment.

The task would need to be one on which the users will make a number of errors; a natural way to achieve this is to present users with a complicated system and invite them to "learn by using." The systems would be identical except with respect to the emotional tone of the error messages. Performance measures called for include: speed of learning, amount of work done, level of satisfaction with the system, and some measure of how likely the user would be to continue to use the system if given the option.

Hypothesis 5: *The user should be alerted to any potentially damaging action.*

On many interactive systems, it is possible with a simple command to cause a good deal of damage. For example, it is often easy to erase input text, delete a file in one's account, or to print pages and pages of text inadvertently. Where there is a possibility of committing such irreversible actions unwittingly, the desirability of alerting the user seems so clear that experiments to prove the point hardly seem necessary. Yet few systems routinely provide such warnings and arguments have been put forth about the annoyance of such warnings to the user who does not want them.

An important contribution that experimentation can make in this area is to define what "potentially damaging" means from a user's point of view. If unnecessary warnings are given frequently, the user may become exasperated with gratuitous messages.

As an initial step, we propose that commands be quantified along a dimension of how much of the user's time would be occupied in undoing them with other commands. For example, the command:

```
DELETE 1000 LINES
```

where no backup file exists would rank very high on such a scale, whereas the command:

```
CHANGE "TBXT" TO "TEXT"
```

would rank low, since it can be easily undone. The experiment is then an attempt to identify where on this scale the benefits of the warning outweigh the annoyance.

Testing this hypothesis requires a series of tasks identical in all respects except for the frequency with which warning messages are given. At one extreme, messages could be given following commands that are very easily undone. On the other extreme, the warning messages would alert the user only to highly "dangerous" commands. The total number of messages would be identical in both cases.

An additional requirement of the design is to evaluate user performance and reaction in situations where the commands actually do have to be undone. Since there is no way of ensuring beforehand that the users will make errors, the design calls for user responses to be monitored and for the system to inform the user after the fact, that the previous command was in error and must be undone.

Thus there are four conditions that define the extreme points of the variables to be examined in this design:

1. a condition in which users are warned about commands that can be easily undone but never actually have to be undone;

2. a condition in which users are warned about commands that would require a great deal of effort to undo but which never actually have to be undone;

3. a condition in which users are not warned about easy-to-undo commands that they subsequently are required to undo;

4. a condition in which users are not warned about difficult-to-undo commands that they are then required to undo.

Performance measures appropriate in this design include amount of work completed and a direct assessment of user satisfaction with the various systems. Obviously, users who are required to undo commands will be able to perform less of the task, but the point of the experiment is to identify that point at which the extra user overhead caused by warning messages is outweighed by the work saved in heeding the warning when it applies.

Hypothesis 6: Error correction should be easy and immediate.

Very little is known about the effect of errors on user performance. In a set of design guidelines, Engel and Granda [1975] indicate that feedback concerning errors should appear in as close proximity, in space and time, as the system will allow. Their observation is, however, that feedback itself is not sufficient for effective user correction.

Many systems give the user the opportunity to edit characters or lines as they are being entered. However, once a line is entered and discovered by the system to be ill-formed, typically the line is lost to the user who must retype it entirely. One exception to this is found in the Pascal Assistant discussed in Chapter 3. With this system, if the user types an ill-formed command, the system immediately brings attention to this fact and permits editing of the offending line. Following such editing, the command is automatically re-executed.

Of greatest concern is the problem of errors arising from commands whose effect is only discovered as erroneous much later. For example, a user may be reorganizing the pages in a file, and when the task is nearly complete may discover that one of the pages was overwritten. While there are schemes for dealing with such errors (for example, maintaining a record of all commands), they are generally quite rare.

One experiment on correction procedures would involve measuring user performance with two systems, identical in all respects except for the error correction mechanism. One system might reject all ill-formed commands and require the user to retype them, as is the case on most systems. The other would allow editing of the ill-formed commands. Dependent measures would include overall user performance, error rates, and efficiency.

We suspect that user errors during interactive computing are not randomly distributed throughout working sessions, but tend to come in bunches. An initial error seems to trigger a series of errors. We speculate that part of the cause may be the sense of frustration caused by the initial error and the difficulty in recovering from it. If our speculation is correct, the cost to the user of an error is not confined to the erroneous command. It also leads to poorer performance in commands issued immediately following. We propose to find empirical verification for this speculation by a sequential analysis of error patterns, applying appropriate statistical tests to show that they occur in groups. Even this would not establish the speculation, however, for it could be that users tend to become generally confused at certain points during a working session and make most of their errors at those times.

Testing the present hypothesis is obviously complex. But in an area as important as this, even some sharp insight would be a contribution. One clear test would be to analyze error rates and their distribution immediately following an initial error. We speculate that easier error correction will improve performance in itself and in addition reduce the probability of errors in subsequent commands.

7.3   Hypotheses Concerning Command Formats

These final hypotheses concern the most effective formats for individual commands. Several issues are addressed: abbreviation rules, command flexibility, and presentation of instructions.

Hypothesis 7:   Command abbreviation rules should be consistent and simple.

Almost all interactive systems employ mnemonic command names and allow some form of abbreviation. As an example, consider the following abbreviations:

```
E       for   END
ERASE   for   ERASE
EX      for   EXIT
```

taken from a commercially available system. Here there is no consistent rule determining the abbreviations and the user must memorize them individually. Our contention is that a consistent abbreviation rule will contribute to better user performance, primarily (but not exclusively) by reducing the effort in memorizing the abbreviations and in reducing the number of errors in entering the abbreviated commands. Some empirical support for our claim is provided by Hodge and Pennington [1972], who showed that, in an abbreviation construction task, subjects performed well using a consistent abbreviation rule.

There are many consistent rules for abbreviation. By consistent we mean that the rule can be stated unambiguously and simply. For example, some rules are:

1. the first N letters,

2. the first dictionary syllable,

3. minimum sequence of letters giving a unique abbreviation to all members of a set of names,

4. deletion of all interior vowels.

All these rules have been used in some way and certain systems use more than one simultaneously.

In addition to being consistent, we speculate that abbreviation rules should be simple. Although we cannot define this concept exactly, we mean that it should be easy for the user to devise the abbreviation by a simple mechanical process. Thus, rule (3) above is not simple to apply because the user must examine and compare every command in a set. Rule (2) is also not simple because it requires a knowledge of syllables. The simplest rule we are aware of is abbreviation to the first letter (see also the next hypothesis).

Verification of this hypothesis can be achieved by a comparison of user performance under systems identical in all respects except for the abbreviations of commands. Designing such an experiment would require considerable ingenuity to avoid confounding variables, such as number of letters in the various abbreviations, phonetic confusibility of letters, and visual confusibility of letters.

To test the consistency portion of the hypothesis, two versions of a text editor could be used. In one, all abbreviations could be formed according to a consistent and simple rule, for example, abbreviation to the first three letters. In the second editor, various rules would be used simultaneously. The sets would be constrained to have the same average number of letters per abbreviation. In addition to recording overall performance, the design would call for special attention to errors made with the command abbreviations.

Hypothesis 8: First-letter abbreviation of command words is a superior abbreviation scheme.

Intuitively, the most easily remembered and reconstructed abbreviation is the first letter of a word. The popularity of first-letter mnemonics attests to this.

Single first-letter commands are undesirable for a number of reasons, however. Engel and Granda [1975] advise never allowing the user to issue important, potentially damaging commands with a single keystroke. Further, the use of first letters only often means that less appropriate synonyms must be substituted for otherwise highly descriptive commands because of overlap of first letters in the command set.

These difficulties may be avoided by grouping the commands into categories and expressing them as phrases. For example, rather than use the following commands:

```
TOP              --  move the current line to the top of the file
BOTTOM           --  move the current line to end of file
TRANSFER         --  transfer current line to buffer
BUFFER           --  insert buffer after current line
```

which present abbreviation conflicts, one could use:

```
ASSUME TOP       --  abbreviation AT or A T
ASSUME BOTTOM    --  abbreviation AB or A B
BUFFER LINE      --  abbreviation BL or B L
INSERT BUFFER    --  abbreviation IB or I B
```

where single-letter abbreviations now have a unique meaning. Notice that the meaning of specific letters is determined by their position within the command.

To establish this as an acceptable abbreviation scheme, an experiment is needed in which user performance is compared under a number of conditions. The results would probably have the greatest impact if a popular, commercially available text editor was used as a model, especially one where the commands tend to be words or phrases. The experiment would involve altering the editing commands so that all commands could be abbreviated by first letters, according to the example given above. Performance on the two editors would then be compared. As a control, it would be necessary to use a third editor, with commands identical to those in the redesigned editor, but with an inconsistent abbreviation scheme. This control condition is necessary to ensure that performance differences would be due to the abbreviation schemes, not to the altered (unabbreviated) commands.

Hypothesis 9: Command languages should be based on legitimate English phrases composed of familiar descriptive words.

Although the completed human engineering experiment described earlier in Chapter 5 strongly supported one aspect of the hypothesis, there are many other issues to be explored. These include the ordering of phrases and the use of punctuation. Another issue left unresolved in that experiment is the question of asymptotic performance. What do the learning curves for the English and the notational editors look like? Would the striking performance differences persist even after a great deal of practice?

We speculate that a system that is difficult to learn remains difficult to use and will, in addition, be forgotten more quickly. To test this speculation, we propose to conduct a longitudinal study with two groups of users. Subjects will be hired to use the editors on a full-time basis for a week. Performance will be monitored, including amount of work done, editing efficiency, and number of errors made. Then, after a period of two months, the subjects will be recalled for a follow-up testing session to determine how well they have retained their editing skills.

This design will provide information on performance differences between editors over a period of intense use and also give a measure of how well each editor is remembered under conditions of intermittent use.

Hypothesis 10: Commands should be described with examples rather than in generalized form.

Consider the following sets of two methods of describing a command. Each has the effect of moving a line pointer.

(a)   FORWARD (n LINES | ALL LINES)

(b)   FORWARD 6 LINES
      FORWARD ALL LINES

Statement (a) is a logical, general representation of the ways in which this command may be used. It contains characters that are not to be typed as part of the command but are used to indicate alternate possibilities. The meaning of these symbols (parenthesis and vertical bar) can only be determined by reading introductory material in the manual from which the command was taken. The use of "n" is not obvious to individuals unfamiliar with algebra.

By contrast, the examples given in statement (b) above make very clear the manner of use of this command. That any number of lines may be requested is implicit in the specification of an arbitrary number. The commands are presented exactly as they should be typed; they do not contain any "meta characters." Our contention is that, for introductory purposes, statement (b) will allow users to learn a system much more quickly and efficiently.

The verification of this hypothesis involves preparing two user's manuals for a specific system or systems in such a way that the only difference between the manuals is in the method used for specifying command formats. Users would then be required to study and use the system, having at their disposal one of the two sorts of manuals. Since the actual commands are identical in the two conditions, a separate-users design is called for. Appropriate dependent measures are study time required and a set of task performance measures. As an alternative, study time could be limited and measures of system comprehension taken.

Note that this hypothesis refers to the manner in which command formats should be presented for tutorial purposes. The value of the more concise, algebraic form of notation for reference and documentation purposes is not called into question by this hypothesis.

Chapter 8

The Design of Experiments

There is a familiar experimental scenario in computing that goes something like this:

We wish to determine the effect of some feature of interest (for example, the choice of control structures or alignment rules) on user comprehension (for example, on program readability). Subjects are given samples with and without the feature. Performance measures are taken, and show no effect. Conclusion: the feature in question is of dubious importance.

Question: Is the experiment flawed or is the conclusion valid?

8.1 The Logic of Experimentation

Interactive computing is a complex and demanding intellectual activity. Much of this complexity is inherent in the nature of computing itself, but much also stems from a mismatch between the characteristics of specific interactive systems, and the capabilities, limitations, needs, and preferences of the human users. The discipline of human engineering, as applied to the design of interactive software, seeks to optimize human performance by tailoring the software system characteristics to human characteristics. Notice that the emphasis is on optimization of human performance, rather than, for example, system performance.

In general, any aspect of a system that is visible to the user has human engineering implications. This includes the functional capabilities of the system, inter-relationships among commands, the surface appearance of the commands, terminal characteristics, response time, error messages, levels of protection, and so forth. Every one of these characteristics results from a specific or implicit design decision.

All too often design decisions are made without regard to human engineering considerations, with the frequent (but not inevitable) result of a system that is difficult to learn, unpleasant and error prone to use, or providing a level of human performance far below potential.

Even assuming a designer placed highest priority on human engineering a particular system, where would he or she turn for information? There is a vast literature dealing with human thought processes, problem solving abilities, and other characteristics that seems to be related to the skills used in interactive computing. The difficulties with access to this literature are many however. Most of us do not have the training to locate and interpret findings that relate to specific design questions. Even given this training, the literature does not contain a widely accepted and carefully cross-indexed set of solutions to specific design problems.

Even beyond these problems, interactive computing is somewhat different from those of other learning and performance tasks. Many of the findings in applied psychology can be extrapolated to the interactive computing situation only with extreme care. Indeed, the study of results in the behavioral sciences deserves a serious research effort on its own. These guidelines, if somewhat uncertain, are valid design tools in human as in other forms of engineering.

We are concerned here with another means for answering design questions, one that provides a rational, reproducible basis for resolving design issues, a means that is open to public scrutiny. This is the area of experimentation, now beginning to become popular in computer science.

In conducting an experiment, one attempts to create a controlled setting in which observation is possible. Interest is not so much in what happens in the experimental situation itself, but rather in what one can generalize from the experimental setting to other similar situations. Experimentation is much like simulation. An attempt is made to create a situation as much like some "goal" situation as possible, or better, to examine two or more alternative situations. The key is in arranging the situations and methods of observation in such a way that the results are readily interpretable.

In a typical experimental situation, data are collected from each of two different settings. If the data from the two settings differ reliably in some way, then one can ascribe the differences as being due to the differences in the settings. The key question is, in what ways did the settings differ? If, in fact, they differed in one and only one way, then it may be fairly conclusive that the difference is responsible for the observed difference in the data.

In practice it almost never happens that two situations are absolutely identical except for one identifiable difference.

To take an example, suppose that a company wants to decide which of two interactive systems for posting and retrieving data to buy. An experiment is arranged in which ten members of the accounting department use system A for a trial period, while ten other members of the accounting department use system B. After the trial period, improvement in work performance is evaluated.

By randomly assigning individuals to groups and by using techniques of statistical inference, the experimenter can assign a *probability* to the possibility that any observed differences are simply due to chance factors (such as, chance differences between the two groups of accountants). If that probability is sufficiently small then the experimenter may be willing to conclude that the differences are actually due to the different systems.

The problem of generalizability can be solved by repeating the entire experiment with another group, say the purchasing department. Notice that this involves a doubling of effort and cost associated with performing the experiment. In fact, the general rule is that the more information wanted from an experiment, the more it is going to cost.

8.2   Designing an Experiment

Before turning to the specifics of experimental design, we must mention two prerequisite conditions that must be met in order to conduct research in this area.

(1)   A meaningful hypothesis must be devised.   Any question to be investigated must stem from a meaningful, carefully stated hypothesis. It must be general enough to have applicability and importance in the intended area of application. There must be some reason for doing the research other than as a purely academic exercise. No amount of technical excellence in carrying out and interpreting an experiment can make up for an hypothesis that is fundamentally unimportant or poorly thought out.

At the same time, the question to be resarched must be narrow and focused enough that it can be couched in testable terms. Many interesting questions can be phrased so broadly that a lifetime of research would be necessary to investigate them thoroughly. Essentially, a single experiment can only answer a single, fairly limited question. In addition, an experiment must be specific enough so that the results can be applied to specific situations.

This initial phrasing of the question in terms that are at once general enough to be important and at the same time specific enough to be testable is probably the most difficult aspect of the whole research enterprise. It follows that a considerable portion of the resources available for the project should be assigned to this phase of the research.

(2) It must be possible to simulate live operation. Given an appro-priate hypothesis, the goal of an experimental project is to provide the conditions implied by the hypothesis on an actual system. Thus it must be possible to simulate the interactive system under consideration. The experimental setting must be as close as possible to the conditions of actual use anticipated for the final product. Without this, the basis for inference to other situations is lost.

It follows that for work of this sort, an all-purpose "system simulation" software package can be an extremely useful, if not an indispensable, tool.

Types of Designs

Once a hypothesis has been formulated it must be cast into a specific experimental design. This aspect of the task ranges from constructing the overall design and planning for the statistical analysis, down to spelling out, in minute detail, all aspects of the procedures to be followed and the measurements to be taken.

The more general aspects of the design are constrained to a large extent by statistical considerations. The involvement of someone experienced in inferential statistics and experimental design is crucial at this point. It is quite possible to design a complex and elegant appearing experiment that, after the fact, turns out to be totally uninterpretable.

Inferential statistics enter because in almost every case our interest is not so much in what exactly happened in one particular experiment, but rather in the question: Given this result, what can be inferred about larger populations? If users with system A outperformed users with system B, would the difference in performance remain if the experiment were repeated or the products released to the general public?

We can do little more here than mention that a large body of established knowledge on the design and interpretation of experiments exists and that a fair amount of specialized training is necessary to use this information effectively. However, below is a brief discussion of some of the experimental designs that are especially useful in work with interactive software.

Single-user class studies.   One of the simplest types of studies involves collecting performance data from a single class of user at a single point in time. Such a study might be used, for example, to decide which of two versions of a text editor give better performance. In such a study, two groups of users might be randomly selected from a pool of users representing the sort of individuals for whom the product is ultimately intended. Individuals in both groups might be given a short training period and then asked to use one of the editors to perform a specific editing task. The procedure would be absolutely identical for each group except that each would work with one of the editors. Performance measurements typically might include: (1) a measure of how much editing was completed in a set period of time, (2) the percentage of erroneous commands issued, and (3) a measure of how efficiently the editing commands were used. At the conclusion of the experiment, the two editors could be compared on the basis of these and possibly other measures. Assuming a clear and statistically reliable result, the experiment would provide a rationale basis for producing, purchasing, or installing the favored editor.

Multiple-user class studies. Very often it is not sufficient to gather data using only a single class of user. For example, the needs of computer naive individuals are very different from those of experienced programmers. A system tailored to one might be inappropriate for the other group. An extension of the single-user class study is the multiple-user class study, in which the experiment is essentially repeated N times using N separate groups of users. As before, each group must be randomly selected from its corresponding population. The populations themselves may be defined by the attributes of interest to the experimenter, but for successful interpretation of results it is critical that the users in the respective populations differ *only* with respect to the variables of interest.

As a simple example, suppose inexperienced and sophisticated programmers are being compared. Assume that the experienced programmers are all successful in their programming careers, whereas the inexperienced individuals are inexperienced precisely because they have no aptitude for programming. In this situation, degree of programming experience is *confounded* with programming aptitude. In analyzing the results, it will be impossible to say whether degree of experience or aptitude was the relevant variable. Such a shortcoming could have serious consequences depending on the group for which the ultimate product is intended.

Longitudinal studies. When a user variable of interest is something that can be acquired by users over time, such as experience, it is possible to employ a powerful design. In a *longitudinal* study the same individuals are tested repeatedly at different points in time. For example, groups of individuals might be tested on each of two editors at the very beginning of their first programming course and then retested after completing the course. The power in the design stems from the fact that each individual is tested twice and, in effect, serves as his or her own control. The problem of confounding of experience and aptitude mentioned above does not arise with the longitudinal design. The main disadvantage of longitudinal designs is that they are time consuming and costly to execute; the design is, however, the method of choice when resources permit.

A major application of the longitudinal design is for studying training and asymptotic performance. When a user is first introduced to a system, his or her performance is usually very different from what it will be after familiarization with and extensive use of the system. The longitudinal study can be used to monitor these changes by evaluating user performance repeatedly at intervals during the familiarization process. Given sufficient experience, performance tends to stabilize; the longitudinal study can be used to determine when performance characteristics approach an asymptote.

Separate-users designs.   A separate-users experiment is one in which separate groups of subjects participate, either because of their individual characteristics or by being assigned to different experimental conditions.

A multiple-user experiment is by definition also a separate-users experiment because separate groups of users are being tested. The separate-users design can also be used in a single-user class experiment. In this case, different users are assigned to the different experimental conditions. In the example given above, systems are being compared. The separate-users design calls for one group of users to use one of the systems, while another group uses the other. In this design, it is important that the separate groups of users be randomly chosen from a larger group of users that have the characteristics of the type of user for whom the product is ultimately intended. If the user groups differ in some systematic way, the experimental results will be confounded.

Same-users design.   The alternative to the separate-users design is the same-users design. With this design, the *same* group of users participates in a variety of experimental conditions. Again referring to the example editor experiment, a same-users design would call for a single group of users to use both of the systems.

A major problem with this design is that the users, having participated in one experimental condition (e.g. using the first system) may now respond differently during the second experimental condition (e.g. using the second system) than they would have without the previous experience. For this reason, it is standard procedure with a same-users design to *counter-balance* the order of the experimental conditions. This counter-balancing also makes it possible to extract statistical information on the effects of *order of presentation* on the user's performance, independent of the effects of the different experimental conditions.

Comparison of Designs

The separate-user design is conceptually simple and straightforward to analyze. In many cases, it is the only option because the experimenter wishes to study different user characteristics that are only found in physically different users. The main disadvantages of the design are that it is costly, requiring a large number of subjects (a separate group for each experimental conditon), and that it is relatively inefficient.

The same-users design is conceptually somewhat more complicated but is more efficient than the separate-users design. In any study, there will be some difference in performance measures between the various groups. In the separate-users design, this performance difference will reflect whatever the true differences between the experimental conditions are (i.e. the extent to which one editor is really superior) but, in addition, much of the observed difference will be due simply to error of measurement and experimental noise. Such experimental noise can obscure the true differences between the experimental conditions. In the separate-users study, much of the noise comes from the simple fact that different individuals are in the different groups.

The same-users design eliminates one major source of experimental noise: the individual differences between the users. This is because each user contributes data to all the experimental conditions; each user serves as his or her own control. With the separate-users design, the total performance difference between, say, two editors will be affected by whatever real difference exists between the editors and also by whatever chance differences happen to exist between the individuals in the groups. In the same-users equivalent, these individual differences do not appear because the same users are in both groups.

Thus the same-users design tends to be more precise — if a true difference exists among the experimental conditions, a same-users design has a better chance of confirming that fact. Conversely, the same-users design can achieve the same level of precision as the separate-users design but with a smaller investment of effort (fewer users required as subjects). In addition to the advantage of precision, the same-users design is the natural choice for a longitudinal study.

Dependent Measures

The experimental design should include detailed plans for what data are to be gathered and how these are to be analyzed. Measures should relate in a clear and obvious way to the hypothesis under consideration. In addition, the measures should be selected to give maximum discriminating power.

Typically, the raw data will consist of a complete record of the user's interaction with the computer including all commands issued, all overstrikes and mistypings, and the time of issue of each command. If the experiment requires the user to perform a task, a record of task performance should be kept.

In addition to performance data that can be recorded automatically, it may be advantageous to obtain information from the users themselves, for example, impressions of the system under study and the experiment in general. This information may be taken as part of the design, in which case a questionnaire should be given that allows the users to respond along a quantitative scale. In addition, any experiment should include a provision for recording general comments and impressions from the users; these can provide valuable insights for interpretation of the results and for designing further experiments.

Any measure should be designed to give maximum discriminability between users and conditions. As an example, suppose that users are to attempt an editing task. One method of scoring their performance might be to record whether or not they finished the task. This measure lumps the users into only two categories. A continuous measure, such as percentage of task completed, will give a much clearer indication of performance differences between conditions.

For similar reasons, time-limited tasks should be designed so that virtually no users will be able to complete them. The experiment will yield the greatest amount of information when the spread of scores across users and conditions is as great as possible. If, for example, 50% of the users are able to complete 100% of an experimental task, it is not possible to differentiate among those users. Performance differences among such users would become more evident given a more difficult task. Whenever more individuals attain the highest possible score on an experimental task, information has been lost because the limits of the users abilities have not been measured.

Importantly, the simpler the measure and the more directly related it is to the hypothesis under consideration, the easier it will be to interpret. Complex measures or those that rely on questionable assumptions for their meaning should be carefully avoided. Straightforward measures, such as percentage of a task completed or number of errors made, will contribute to the understandability and favorable impact of any result.

8.3   Preparing to Execute an Experiment

The purpose of conducting an experiment is to create the opportunity for controlled observation in a manner that allows inferences to be made to other situations. As with simulation techniques, it is important that the experimental situation closely model the situations about which inferences are to be drawn.

The most variable parameters in interactive computing are those represented by the users. Interactive computing is a highly idiosyncratic activity; individuals tend to have their own strongly personal computing styles. For example, given an editing task, some users will work from the start of the text to the end, making all the corrections as they go. Others may make all corrections of one sort (e.g. letter or word substitutions) first, then all corrections of another sort (e.g. line additions and transpositions), and so on. Still other users may prefer starting at the end of the text and working backward. Other variables that affect user performance include: level of experience, attitude towards computers, understanding of the potential of computer power, type of task the user needs to accomplish, general intelligence, dexterity, motivation, and education.

Given this extreme variability in computing style and performance, it is critical to analyze the experimental user population as carefully as possible, and to select individuals who are as similar as possible to the type of user for whom the system being designed is ultimately intended.

Finally, unless the subjects chosen for the experiment are a random sampling of individuals from the larger population about which it is desired to make inferences, then the statistical basis for such inference is lost. It follows that considerable effort and care should be taken to ensure random sampling.

Pilot Testing

Even the simplest experiment is a complicated and time-consuming undertaking. Many details of the experimental procedure simply cannot be anticipated prior to actual execution of the experiment. For a start, software may fail. If the experiment is to be run on a time-sharing system, system load may become an important consideration. Subjects are certain to ask questions unless specifically prohibited. To what extent should these be answered during the experimental session? How fully should the subjects be informed of the nature of the experiment? It may well become evident during the course of experimentation that the users are interpreting the task in a totally different way from that intended by the experimenter.

It is unrealistic to expect to anticipate all the problems related to the design of the experiment. Thus an essential phase in executing the experiment is the pilot test. The purpose of this is not only to gather information on the experimental hypothesis, but to practice and examine the experimental procedures for flaws. A secondary purpose is to see if there is sufficient reason to pursue the experiment at all.

Thus the pilot test is a preliminary dry run for the experiment itself. The same care and attention to detail that will go into the experiment should also be exercised in planning and executing the pilot test. However, in the experiment itself, the details of the procedure must *never* be changed while the experiment is in progress. By contrast, the pilot phase is an appropriate time to try hunches, modify procedures, and change aspects of the design that seem not to be working as intended.

At the conclusion of the pilot test phase there should exist an experimental design and set of experimental procedures that spell out in *complete detail* exactly what the final shape of the experiment is to be and precisely what procedures are to be followed. Thus the exact number of users to be tested will be known along with explicit plans for sampling the user population. Any written or spoken material that is to be presented to the users will be planned for. The experimental procedures will have actually been administered to a number of individuals without problems or uncertainties arising.

Given this level of planning, the actual administration of the experiment merely involves carefully and faithfully executing the predetermined plans. Any deviation or alteration of procedures during the execution of the experiment involves the risk of invalidating the entire effort.

8.4   Problems and Cautions

We close this chapter with a number of points brought out in the diary of Chapter 6.

Considering Alternatives

During the design phase, it is easy to underestimate the number of different approaches to the problem. In an endeavor of this sort, the assumptions that one makes early on have a way of exerting an immutable influence for the duration of the project. The mere fact that a large effort has been invested in some aspect of the design is no justification for keeping it. Learning to question all aspects of the design is not easy. We must not be afraid to scrap portions of the design if a better idea presents itself.

There should be an explicit reason for every feature of an experimental design. If there is no particular reason for some aspect of a design or procedure, there is a good reason for re-examining that aspect. As an example, consider an experiment in which two text editors are to be compared. One procedural question is: what actual text are the users to edit during the experiment? At first glance it might seem that any text would do. In fact, selection of an appropriate sort of text can be quite important to the success of the experiment. Lines of program code, for example, would be quite unsuitable unless one could be sure that all the users were equally familiar (or unfamiliar) with the programming language. Ordinary prose may have drawbacks too, especially if it is interesting enough to distract the user's attention from the editing task.

Bias

A major problem in any experiment is *bias*. Opportunities for prejudicing results abound in all aspects of experimentation from design to interpretation of results. Even worse, an experimenter can bias an experiment quite unconsciously; in fact, probably most instances of experimental bias are unknown to the perpetrators.

Perhaps the most subtle form of bias arises in the initial framing of the experimental question. That is, the question itself may be phrased in such a way as to favor a particular class of answer. In the scientific community, where research results and the methodology giving rise to them are public knowledge, a fair amount of time is spent in questioning each assumption so that bias of this sort is likely to be brought to attention. In an industry or a military setting, however, this corrective mechanism cannot operate as effectively and the problem is likely to be greater.

Possibilities for biasing the results exist in the selection of procedures and in the recruiting of subjects. Such bias is usually called *confounding*. As an example, suppose that in a comparison of two systems, the users of one have more experience than the users of the other. One cannot readily conclude whether the results were due to the differences between the systems or to the experience levels of the subjects.

The experimenter can bias the results in the way he or she treats the subjects. Unconscious bias is a real possibility here. In a comparison of systems, the experimenter may unintentionally communicate to the users a preference for one of the systems, and this may influence their performance. In medical research with experimental drugs, a technique known as the "double-blind procedure" is sometimes used to eliminate all possibility of problems of this sort. In a double-blind procedure neither the experimenter nor the subjects knows what experimental condition they are involved in. Such a design is particularly appropriate in the comparison of an experimental pain reliever with a placebo, for example.

In software experiments, it is usually impossible to conceal the conditions from the experimenter and users but there are some precautions that can be taken:

1. Automating the data-taking procedures.

2. Standardizing the instructions.

3. Where possible, giving the subjects written as opposed to spoken instructions (unfortunately, written instructions tend to be less effective in explaining complex tasks so a trade-off is involved here).

4. Not giving the user any unnecessary information about the purposes and design of the experiment.

However, these precautions should not be carried so far as to create an unfriendly, unmotivating, or confusing situation for the subjects. The success of the experiment will depend on their enthusiasm, understanding of the task, and cooperation.

Rights of Human Subjects

In all experimental situations there is a moral, and in most situations, a legal obligation to take all reasonable steps to ensure the rights of human subjects in research. There is no universally agreed upon set of guidelines designed to achieved this end, but *any* research performed in a college or university setting must have met the approval of an institutional research review board. This is true whether or not the research is federally funded.

At a minimum the rights of subjects in research include the following:

1. To be fully informed of the nature of the research as it pertains to their physical and psychological well being;

2. To be free of harrassment, embarrassment, humiliation, or physical risk;

3. To be assured of the confidentiality of information and data taken from them during the research;

4. To be free to terminate their participation in the experiment at any time for any reason or no reason;

5. To be informed of their rights as subjects in research.

In any research project, a written statement should be given to the subject, detailing the purposes of the research, what will be done to the subject, a description of the subject's rights, and a clear statement of any possible harm that may befall the subject as consequence of the experiment. If the subject agrees to participate in the research, he or she should then be asked to sign a "statement of informed consent" giving agreement to participate after being informed of the purposes of the research, their rights, and any associated risks.

In any university or government setting, and increasingly in industry, there will be an institutional review board whose function it is to review proposed experiments with regard to the rights of subjects. Fortunately, most experiments in interactive software design will involve no risk to the subjects.

The Null Result

Let us return to the question posed at the beginning of this chapter.

We wish to determine the effect of some feature of interest (for example, the choice of control structures or alignment rules) on user comprehension (for example, on program readability). Subjects are given samples with and without the feature. Performance measures are taken, and show no effect. Conclusion: the feature in question is of dubious importance.

Question: Is the experiment flawed or is the conclusion valid?

There are many sources of "noise" in an experiment and it is all too easy to conclude that the feature in question shows no significant performance effect. The best experiments will show precisely the true effect, and when differences are reported, the results are difficult to assail. But when *no* differences are found, a much stronger case must be made before that result can be accepted with confidence. A null result should always be questioned.

References

[Aho and Johnson 1974]
A. V. Aho and S. C. Johnson
LR Parsing
Computing Surveys, June 1974

[Anderson and Gillogly 1976]
R. H. Anderson and J. J. Gillogly
Rand Intelligent Terminal Agent (RITA): Design Philosophy
No. R-1809-ARPA, Rand Corporation, Santa Monica, CA, 1975

[Bailey et.al. 1973]
Robert W. Bailey, Stephen T. Demers, and Allen I. Lebowitz
Human Reliability in Computer-based Business Information Systems
IEEE Transactions on Reliability, August 1973

[Baker and Goldstein 1966]
J. D. Baker and I. Goldstein
Batch vs Sequential Displays: Effects on human problem solving
Human Factors, Vol 8, 1966

[Birmingham and Taylor 1954]
H. P. Birmingham and F. V. Taylor
A Design Philosophy for Man-machine Control Systems
Proceedings of the I.R.E, Vol. XLII, 1954

178   References

[Boies 1974]
Stephen J. Boies
User Behavior on an Interactive Computer System
IBM Systems Journal, January 1974

[Boies and Gould 1974]
Stephen J. Boies and John D. Gould
Syntactic Errors in Computer Programming
Human Factors, Vol. 16(3), 1974

[Brooks 1975]
Ruven Brooks
A Model of Human Cognitive Behavior Code for Computer Programs
Ph.D dissertation, Carnegie-Mellon University, Pittsburgh, PA, 1975

[Burks et al. 1946]
A. W. Burks, H. H. Goldstein, and J. von Neumann
Preliminary Discussion of the Logical Design of an Electronic
        Computing Instrument
In A. H. Taub (editor) *Collected Works of Jon von Neumann* 5: 34-79,
        The MacMillan Company, New York, 1946.

[Caldwell 1975]
John Caldwell
The Effective Reports Crisis
Journal of Systems Management, June 1975

[Campbell and Stanley 1963]
D. T. Campbell and Julian C. Stanley
Experimental and Quasi-experimental Designs for Research
Rand McNally College Publishing Company, Chicago, 1963

[Carlisle 1974]
J. H. Carlisle
Man-computer Interactive problem Solving: Relationships between
        user characteristics and interface complexity
Ph.D. dissertation, Yale University, 1974

[Child et al. 1961]
Julia Child, L. Bertholle, and S. Beck
Mastering the Art of French Cooking I
Alfred A. Knopf, New York, 1961

[Churchill 1956]
A. V. Churchill
The Effect of Scale Interval Length and Pointer Clearance on Speed
        and Accuracy of Interpolation
Journal of Applied Psychology, 40, 1956, p. 358-361

[CMS 1976]
CMS Users Guide
IBM Virtual Machine Facility, Release 3
IBM, Burlingto MA, 1976

[Conrad 1967]
R. Conrad
Designing Postal Codes for Public Use
In W.T. Singleton et al. (editors) *The Human Operator in
     Complex Systems*
     Taylor and Francis, Ltd., London, 1967

[Conway 1963]
Melvin Conway
Design of a Separable Transition-Diagram Compiler
Communications of the ACM, Vol. 6(7), 1963

[Cooke and Bunt 1975]
J. E. Cooke and R. B. Bunt
Human Error in Programming: The need to study the individual
     programmer
Department of Computational Science Technical Report 75-3,
     University of Saskatchewan, Canada, 1975

[Cuadra 1971]
Carlow A. Cuadra
On-Line Systems: Promise and Pitfalls
Journal of the American Society for Information Science,
     March-April, 1971

[Edwards 1954]
W. Edwards
The Theory of Decision Making
Psychological Bulletin, Vol. 51, 1954

[Embley 1976]
David W. Embley
Experimental and Formal Language Design Applied to Control Constructs
     for Interactive Computing
Department of Computer Science Technical Report No. UIUCDCS-R-76-811,
     University of Illinois, Urbana, 1976

[Engel and Granda 1975]
S. E. Engel and R. E. Granda
Guidelines for Man/Display Interfaces
IBM Poughkeepsie Laboratory Technical Report No. TR00.27200, 1975

[Epstein and Arlinsky 1965]
W. Epstein and M. Arlinsky
The Interaction of Syntactical Structure and Learning Instructions
Psychological Science, March 3, 1965

[Ferster and Skinner 1957]
C. B. Ferster and B. F. Skinner
Schedules of Reinforcement
Appleton-Century-Crofts, New York, 1957

[Freedman and Landauer 1966]
J. L. Freedman and T. K. Landauer
Retrieval of Long-Term Memory: Tip-of-the-tongue Phenomenon
Psychological Science, August 1966

[Gannon and Horning 1975]
John D. Gannon and James J. Horning
Language Design for Programming Reliability
IEEE Transactions on Software Engineering, Vol. SE-1(2), 1975

[Gilb and Weinberg 1977]
Thomas Gilb and Gerald Weinberg
Humanized Input: Techniques for Reliable Keyed Input
Winthrop Publishers, Cambridge MA, 1977

[Gould et al. 1971]
John D. Gould, Walter J. Doherty, and Stephen J. Boies
Bibliography of Behavioral Aspects of On-line Computer Programming
IBM Watson Research Center Technical Report RC-3513
Yorktown Heights, NY, August 1971

[Gould and Drongowski 1974]
John D. Gould and Paul Drongowski
An Exploratory Study of Computer Program Debugging
Human Factors, Vol. 16(3), 1974

[Grignetti et al. 1975]
M. Grignetti, J. Gould, and C. Hausmann
NLS-Scholar: Modifications and Field Testing, ESD-TR-75-358
Bolt, Bernaek, and Newman, Inc., Cambridge MA, 1975

[Grossberg et al. 1976]
Mitchell Grossberg, Raymond A. Wiesen, and Douive B. Yntema
An Experiment on Problem Solving with Delayed Computer Responses
IEEE Transactions on Systems, Man, and Cybernetics, March 1976

[Hoare 1969]
C.A.R. Hoare
An Axiomatic Basis for Computer Programming
Communications of the ACM, Vol. 12(10), 1969

[Hoare and Wirth 1973]
C.A.R. Hoare and Niklaus Wirth
An Axiomatic Definition of the Programming Language Pascal
Acta Informatica 2, 1973, Springer-Verlag

[Hodge and Pennington 1973]
M. H. Hodge and F. M. Pennington
Some Studies of Word Abbreviation Behavior
Journal of Experimental Psychology, Vol. 98, 1973

[Holt and Stevenson 1977]
H. O. Holt and F. L. Stevenson
Human Performance Considerations in Complex Systems
Science, May 1977

[Hueras and Ledgard 1977]
Jon Hueras and Henry Ledgard
An Automatic Formatting Program for Pascal
Sigplan Notices, July 1977

[Jensen and Wirth 1974]
Kathleen Jensen and Niklaus Wirth
Pascal User Manual and Report: Lecture Notes in Computer Science 18
Springer-Verlag, New York, 1974

[Johnson 1967]
E. A. Johnson
Touch Displays: A Programmed Man-Machine Interface
Ergonomics, Vol. 10(2), 1967

[Kennedy 1974]
T.C.S. Kennedy
The Design of Interactive Procedures for Man-Machine Communication
International Journal of Man-Machine Studies, Vol. 5, 1974

[Kennedy and Van Cott 1972]
J. S. Kennedy and H. P. Van Cott
System and Human Engineering Analyses
In H.P. Van Cott and R. Kinkade (editors) *Human Engineering Guide
      to Equipment Design* US GPO, Doc. D4.10:EN3
Washington D.C., 1972

182 References

[Lathwell and Mezei 1971]
R. H. Lathwell and J. E. Mezei
A Formal Description of APL
Colloque APL, Paris, 1971

[Lawson et al. 1978]
H. W. Lawson, Jr. M. Bertran and J. Sanagustin
The Formal Definition of Human/Machine Communications
Software — Practice and Experience, August 1978

[Ledgard and Hueras 1976]
Henry Ledgard and Jon Hueras
A Semi-formal Definition of the Assistant's Editor
Private communication

[Ledgard 1977]
Henry Ledgard
Production Systems: A Notation for Defining Syntax and Translation
        of Programming Languages
IEEE Transactions on Software Engineering, March, 1977

[Ledgard et al. 1978]
Henry Ledgard, Andrew Singer, Jon Hueras, and Daryl Winters
A User's Guide to HOPE — A Human Oriented Program Editor
Computer and Information Science Department Technical Report 78-05
        University of Massachusetts, Amherst, 1978

[Ledgard 1980]
Henry Ledgard
A Human Engineered Variant of BNF
Sigplan Notices, 1980

[Love 1977]
Thomas Love
An Experimental Investigation of the Effect of Program Structure
        on Program Understanding
Sigplan Notices, March 1977

[Mann 1977]
J. Mann
Decision Making
The Free Press, New York, 1977

[Mann 1975]
William Mann
Why Things Are So Bad for the Computer-naive User
Proceedings of the National Computer Conference, 1975

[Marcotty et al. 1976]
Michael Marcotty, Henry Ledgard, and Gregor Bochmann
A Sampler of Formal Definitions
Computing Surveys, June 1976

[Martin 1973]
J. Martin
Design of Man-Computer Dialogues
Prentice Hall, New Jersey, 1973

[McCullough 1972]
D. McCullough
The Great Bridge
Avon Books, New York, 1972

[Miller 1956]
George A. Miller
The Magical Number Seven Plus or Minus Two: Some Limits on Our
        Capacity for Processing Information
Psychological Review,63, 1956

[Miller and Thomas 1977]
Lance Miller and J. C. Thomas
Behavioral Issues in the Use of Interactive Systems: Part I, General
        System Issues
Thomas J. Watson Research Center, Yorktown Heights NY, 1977

[Miller 1974]
Lance Miller
Programming by Non-programmers
Journal of Man-Machine Studies, Vol. 6, 1974

[Miller and Becker 1974]
Lance Miller and Curtis Becker
Programming in Natural English
IBM Research, RC5137, Yorktown Heights, NY, 1974

[Miller 1975]
Lance Miller
Naive Programmer Problems with Specification of Transfer-of-Control
Proceedings of National Computer Conference, AFIPS, Vol. 44, 1975

[Miller 1976]
Laurence Miller
An Investigation of the Effects of Output Variability and Output
        Bandwidth on User Performance in an Interactive Computer System
ISI/RR-76-50, ARPA Order No. 2223, Information Sciences Institute,
        Marina Del Rey, CA, 1976

[Myers 1966]
Jerome L. Myers
Fundamentals of Experimental Design
Allyn and Bacon, Boston, 1966

[Niggemann 1975]
N. Niggemann
A Method for the Semantic Description of Command Languages
In *Command Languages*, C. Unger (editor)
North-Holland Publishing Co., Amsterdam, 1975

[Parnas 1969]
David Parnas
On the Use of Transition Diagrams in the Design of a User Interface
      for an Interactive Computer System
Proceedings of 1969 National ACM Conference, 1969

[Palme 1975]
J. Palme
Interactive Software for Humans
Research Institute of National Defense NTIS No. PB-245 553
Stockholm, Sweden, 1975

[Parsons 1970]
H. M. Parsons
The Scope of Human Factors in Computer-based Data Processing Systems
Human Factors, Vol. 12(2), 1970

[Ramsey and Atwood 1979]
H. Rudy Ramsey and Michael E. Atwood
Human Factors in Computer Systems: A review of the literature
Technical Report SAI-79-111-DEN, Science Applications Inc. Englewood, CO, 1979

[Riddle 1976]
Elizabeth A. Riddle
A Comparative Study of Various Text Editors and Formatting Systems
Project 0147A, No. AD-A029050, Defense Documentation Center Cameron Station,
Alexandria, VA, August 1976

[Rouse 1975]
W. Rouse
Design of Man-Computer Interfaces for On-line Interactive Systems
Proceedings of the IEEE, Vol. 63(6), 1975

[Sackman 1970]
Harold Sackman
Time-Sharing and Self-Tutoring: An exploratory case history
Human Factors, February 1970

[Seymour 1978]
William Seymour
Diary of a Human Factors Experiment
Computer and Information Science Technical Report 77-14
University of Massachusetts, Amherst, 1978

[Shneiderman 1980]
Benjamin Shneiderman
Software Psychology
Winthrop Publishing Company, Cambridge MA, 1980

[Shneiderman and Mayer 1975]
Benjamin Shneiderman and R. Mayer
Towards a Cognitive Model of Programmer Behavior
Technical Report 37, Indiana University, Bloomington, 1975

[Shneiderman et al. 1977]
Benjamin Shneiderman, R. Mayer, D. McKay, and P. Heller
Experimental Investigations of the Utility of Detailed Flowcharts
        In Programming
Communications of the ACM, June 1977

[Singer 1979]
Andrew Singer
Formal Methods and Human Factors in the Design of Interactive Languages
Ph.D. Dissertation, University of Massachusetts, Amherst, 1979

[Steel 1966]
T. B. Steel, Jr.
Formal Language Description Languages for Computer Programming
In T. B. Steel, Jr. (editor) *Proceedings of the IFIP Working
        Conference on Formal Language Description Languages*
North-Holland Publishing Company, Amsterdam, 1966

[Sterling 1974]
T.D. Sterling
Guidelines for Humanizing Computerized Information Systems: a report
        from Stanley House
Communications of the ACM, November 1974

[Stewart 1976]
T.F.M. Stewart
Displays and the Software Interface
Applied Ergonomics, Vol. 7(3), 1976

186 References

[Teitelman 1974]
W. Teitelman
Interlisp Reference Manual
Xerox Corporation, Palo Alto Research Center, CA, 1974

[Tennent 1976]
R. D. Tennent
The Denotational Semantics of Programming Languages
Communications of the ACM, Vol. 19(8), 1976

[Thomas 1976a]
John C. Thomas
Quantifiers and Question-Asking
IBM Thomas J. Watson Research Center Technical Report RC-5866
Yorktown Heights, NY, 1976

[Thomas 1976b]
John C. Thomas
A Method for Studying Natural Language Dialogue
IBM Thomas J. Watson Research Center Technical Report RC-5882
Yorktown Heights, NY, 1976

[Thomas and Gould 1975]
John C. Thomas and John D. Gould
A Psychological Study of Query by Example
Proceedings of the National Computer Conference, AFIPS, Vol. 44, 1975

[Thorndike and Rock 1934]
E. L. Thorndike and R. T. Rock, Jr.
Learning without Awareness of What is Being Learned or Intent To
      Learn It
Journal of Experimental Psychology, Vol. XVII(1), 1934

[Torrero 1975]
E. A. Torrero
*Focus on Microprocessors in Microprocessors: New directions for
      designers*, E.A. Torrero (editor)
Hayden Publishing Company, New Jersey, 1975

[Turner 1974]
R. Turner
Interaction Data From CS/2
Digital Equipment Corporation, Maynard, MA, 1974

[van Dam and Rice 1971]
Andries van Dam and David E. Rice
On-Line Text Editing: A Survey
Computing Surveys, Vol. 3(3), September 1971

[Vandenberg 1967]
J. D. Vandenberg
Improved Operating Procedures Manuals
Ergonomics, Vol. 10(2), 1967

[van Wijngaarden et al. 1969]
A. van Wijngaarden, B. J. Mailloux, J. E. Peck, and C.H.A. Koster
Report on the Algorithmic Language ALGOL 68
MR 101, Mathematish Centrum, Amsterdam, 1969

[Walther and O'Neil 1974]
G. H. Walther and H. F. O'Neil
On-line User-computer Interface — The effects of Interface Flexibility,
    Terminal Type, and Experience on Performance
AFIPS Conference Proceedings, 1974

[Weinberg 1971]
Gerald Weinberg
The Psychology of Computer Programming
Van Nostrand Reinhold Company, New York, 1971

[Weissman 1974]
Laurence M. Weissman
A Methodology for Studying the Psychological Complexity of Computer
    Programs
Computer Systems Research Group, University of Toronto Technical
    Report CSRG-37, Canada, 1974

[Weist and Dolezal 1972]
R. Weist and J. Dolezal
The Effect of Violating Phrase Structure Rules and Selectional
    Restrictions on TEP Patterns
Psychological Science, June 1972

[Wegner 1972]
Peter Wegner
The Vienna Definition Languge
Computing Surveys, Vol. 4(1), 1972

[Weizenbaum 1976]
J. Weizenbaum
Computer Power and Human Reason
W.H. Freeman and Company, San Francisco, 1976

[Whiteside 1979]
John A. Whiteside
Human Engineering of Interactive Software — An Experimental Study
M.S. thesis, Worcester Polytechnic Institute, 1979

188 References

[Wiedman 1974]
C. Wiedman
Handbook of APL Programming
Petrocelli Books, New York, 1974

[Wilcox et al. 1976]
Thomas Wilcox, Alan M. Davis, and Michael H. Tindall
The Design and Implementation of a Table Driven, Interactive Diagnostic
    Programming System
Communications of the ACM, November 1976

[Wirth 1968]
Niklaus Wirth
A Programming Language for the 360 Computer
Journal of the ACM, Vol. 15, 1968

W. A. Woods
Transition Network Grammars for Natural Language Analysis
Communications of the ACM, Vol 13(10), 1970

[Wright and Barnard 1975]
P. Wright and P. Barnard
Just Fill in This Form – A Review for Designers
Applied Ergonomics, Vol. 6 (4), 1975

[Yasaki 1974]
E. K. Yasaki
The Emerging Micro-Computer
Datamation, December 1974

Index